Edgar Cayce
and
Christian Faith

Edgar Cayce
and
Christian Faith

by Lynn Elwell Sparrow

Revised edition of
Edgar Cayce and the Born Again Christian

ASSOCIATION FOR
RESEARCH AND
ENLIGHTENMENT

A.R.E. Press • Virginia Beach • Virginia

A.R.E. Press
215 67th Street
Virginia Beach, VA 23451-2061

Library of Congress Cataloging-in-Publication Data
Sparrow, Lynn Elwell.
Edgar Cayce and Christian faith / Lynn Elwell Sparrow.
      p. cm.
Rev. ed. of : Edgar Cayce and the born again Christian.
© 1985.
ISBN 0-87604-458-5
1. Cayce, Edgar, 1877-1945. 2. Parapsychology—Religious
aspects—Christianity. I. Sparrow, Lynn Elwell. Edgar Cayce
and the born again Christian. II. Title.
BF1027.C3S63   1999
261.5'13—dc21   99-36480

Cover design by Lightbourne

To Mom and Pop

Contents

Part Four
Reincarnation and Christian Faith

Part Five
Edgar Cayce and the Bible

Appendices

Acknowledgments

Many of the people I wish to thank appear anonymously in the personal account which begins *Edgar Cayce and Christian Faith*. It seems best that they should remain anonymous, for I'm not sure that all of them would welcome public recognition of the influence they have had in shaping my approach to this somewhat controversial subject. However, if any of them read my story, I hope they will recognize themselves and accept my heartfelt thanks for the role they have played in my personal religious experience as well as the development of the thoughts presented here. I particularly want to thank my first pastor and his wife, my two earliest Sunday school teachers, the friends who first gave me *There Is a River,* my original study group "family," the Assembly of God pastor who showed me so much of the workings of the Spirit in this world, the excellent professors at the Christian college I attended, and the many A.R.E. speakers and authors whose works have had such a profound effect on me.

I would also like to thank Bob Clapp, Susan Lendvay, and Elaine Hruska, whose help was invaluable on more than one occasion in tracking down the case number and exact wording of a Cayce reading that I knew only in paraphrased form. Their expertise in researching the readings and their repeated patience in putting that expertise to work on my behalf are gratefully acknowledged here. My thanks go again to Elaine Hruska for the fine and sensitive job she has done in editing this work.

I could not let this opportunity go by without thanking my parents, Phyllis and Ernie Elwell—to whom this book is also dedicated—for their support and encouragement not only during the time that I worked on this book, but during every stage and project of my life. They have given me more help than they'll ever know.

Preface

IN THE TIME since the original version of this work was published under the title, *Edgar Cayce and the Born Again Christian,* there has been a virtual explosion of what might be called "alternative spirituality" in our culture. Growing numbers of people have taken seriously to practices that in times past might have been called "occult." Such diverse phenomena as channeling, past-life exploration, astrology, extraterrestrial revelations, and psychic consultation services that range from the serious intuitive professional to the psychic hotline are now loosely grouped under the heading "New Age." Bestselling books such as *The Celestine Prophecy* and

Conversations with God have taken spiritual philosophies that a few short decades ago would have been considered quite foreign to Western culture and catapulted them into popular awareness. Simultaneously, increased mainstream acceptance of the mind-body connection in matters of physical health, along with the growing popularity of body energy healing therapies, has launched many people on spiritual quests through their use of alternative healing modalities. We live in a time when more people than ever before are seeking their spiritual answers outside the established churches and synagogues. For some, this is seen as evidence of our collective spiritual evolution. To others, it is a lamentable loss of traditional beliefs and values. For those spiritual seekers who find value in *both* the traditional and the "New Age" approaches to spirituality, it is a false dichotomy that unnecessarily divides us.

Perhaps more than ever before, the intuitive readings of Edgar Cayce stand as an influence that keeps us anchored to that which has withstood the changing tides of human thought while at the same time showing us the vast sea of possibilities that is ours to explore. In its seemingly paradoxical Christ-centered-yet-universal framework, the Cayce material challenges us to find new meaning in what it means to embrace a personal faith in Christ while remaining open enough to explore the multitudinous dimensions of God's revelation to and through the human soul. For those of traditional Christian faith, this is often indeed a challenging—if not daunting—undertaking.

From the time *Edgar Cayce and the Born Again Christian* was first published, I have continued to receive letters of appreciation from people all over the world who were drawn to the Cayce material, but sensitive in one way or another about issues involving its compatibility with Christianity. For some it was a matter of resolving inner conflicts. For others it had more to do with external pressure from others in their families or churches. For still others, it was simply a desire to more fully integrate the spiritual edification they received from the Cayce readings with that which they received in their churches and from their Bibles. Despite the book's being out of print for the last several years, requests for it have persisted. To my knowledge there is still no other publication available that is sympathetic to both traditional Christian beliefs and the contemporary spiritual philosophy that Edgar Cayce was so instrumental in introducing to Western culture. This revised and retitled volume has been prepared with the hope that the central issues addressed here may make it just a little more likely that more people will hold fast to their Christian faith while benefiting from insights and practices arising from the burgeoning spiritual awakening in our times.

Any consideration of the cultural milieu into which *Edgar Cayce and Christian Faith* is being introduced must take into account another development since the earlier work's publication. The rise of the "Christian right" as a political force has done strange things to the popular notion of what it means to be a Christian. As vocal proponents of a certain theology-turned-political agenda have been prominently featured in the media, they have come to represent for many non-Christians the essential Christian identity. Consequently, there has been a growing reluctance on the part of those Christians who do not share the political agenda to even be known by the label, "Christian." I found myself chuckling ruefully in going over my analogy in chapter 12 between reincarnation and political party affiliation. In making the case that belief in reincarnation is neither inherently Christian nor inherently non-Christian, I liken it to political party affiliation, which is an add-on choice for a Christian rather than being necessitated by his or her Christianity. In the light of developments in America since I first wrote that, I considered changing my analogy. In the end, however, I opted to keep it. For it is still true that the core Christian faith I am talking about here is not the exclusive property of any one denomination, movement, or sect.

Finding a term that adequately describes that Christian tradition which emphasizes redemptive faith in Jesus Christ and the Bible as the source of spiritual truth remains problematical. It is largely because of the limiting connotations of the label "born again" in the original title that I have replaced it with the more general "Christian faith." For example, Roman Catholics who may have much resonance with the content of the book would not particularly relate to the "born again" label. Throughout the book, I have tried to use a variety of terms in order to emphasize that I do not mean to refer to any one particular group or even a monolithic set of doctrines when I discuss Cayce's compatibility with certain "core" or "fundamental" Christian beliefs. I have used the words, "traditional," "doctrinally conservative," "biblically centered," "biblically based," "fundamental," and "Evangelical" as descriptive of the Christian perspectives I am addressing here. Labels aside, however, I think the reader will recognize the *issues* addressed in *Edgar Cayce and Christian Faith* as the ones which most often get in the way of a Christian's acceptance of Edgar Cayce's rich offerings to our spiritual understanding.

As any writer who undertakes to revise and reissue an earlier work will discover, a book is somewhat like a detailed snapshot: a view of life at a particular point in time. Upon viewing it years later, it is interesting to note what has changed and what has remained the same. In looking at old photos, perhaps clothing and hairstyles show the most dramatic differences. The experiences of the years will almost certainly show up on the faces. But the essential nature of the people in the picture remains the same, despite the passage of time.

Fifteen years have passed since I wrote the original version of this book. The roller-coaster ride of life experiences that often characterize the passage from young adulthood to middle age has brought many learning experiences to me and stretched my thinking into previously uncharted territory. Finding a church home that is less antagonistic to the Cayce material than those I had previously known has lessened the urgency for me personally of "justifying" Cayce to those whose beliefs preclude him. Yet I know that as the influence of what I have called "alternative spirituality" continues to spread, many sincere seekers within the conservative churches will be thrown into the very center of the conflict between the "New Age" and the traditional. The constant for me during these fifteen years of growth and change has been the central importance of staying close to the Master of masters. And the soul-quickening insight and inspiration of the Edgar Cayce readings has continued to be a mainstay in my ongoing quest to know Him more intimately.

My conviction has certainly deepened that the Cayce readings and core Christian beliefs are two entirely compatible ingredients in a maturing spiritual life. In fact, for me, what may have once been mere compatibility has become a synergy wherein the beautifully Christ-centered expression in the Cayce material inspires my Christian faith, and my Christian faith imbues my study of Cayce with deeper meaning. It is this synergy, more than anything else, that I wish to help make possible for others through addressing those core questions at the heart of *Edgar Cayce and Christian Faith*.

Lynn Sparrow
May 1999

Introduction

EDGAR CAYCE, THE most documented psychic in modern history, has often been called a "Christian mystic." Some might consider this an apt description of a man who used his psychic powers not to produce sensational phenomena but to help people who were seeking to understand their relationship with God. Admittedly, Cayce's psychically given information is universal enough to accommodate many religious perspectives. It is not exclusively Christian in the sense that it denies the validity of other religions. Nonetheless, in uniting the tenets of Christianity with the mystical traditions of East and West, the psychic readings of this famous clairvoyant have led countless Christians to a deeper vision of their faith and renewed commitment to their churches.

Yet some of Edgar Cayce's most outspoken critics come from within certain denominations of the church. In fact, it would seem that as the popularity of the Cayce legacy increases, there is a corresponding increase in Christian opposition to it. It is not unusual to find within books which warn Christians to stay away from occult and demonic practices entire chapters devoted to Edgar Cayce. It has become increasingly common for television preachers and Christian talk show guests to name Edgar Cayce when they discuss dangerous and false doctrines. Among some communities of Christian faith, it is even assumed that involvement with the work of Edgar Cayce is a sure sign that one has been deceived by the devil. Why do we find such dire warnings coming from those whom we might have expected to welcome Cayce's emphasis on spiritual values and personal responsibility before God? At the root of most Christian objection to the work of Edgar Cayce, we find the viewpoint that all psychic experience is condemned by the Bible and that the specific information in Cayce's psychic readings contains "teachings" that are antithetical to Christian faith. In the pages to come, we will consider these basic questions as well as related questions that spring from them: Was Edgar Cayce really an instrument of the devil, as some Christians claim? Is the information in his psychic readings damaging to Christian faith, as some well-meaning Christians warn their followers? Indeed, *is* it impossible to be a Bible-believing Christian and maintain an involvement with the work of Edgar Cayce or the Association for Research and Enlightenment (A.R.E.), the organization founded to study his psychic readings?

Debates over these questions are often clouded with misunderstandings on both sides. The Christians who warn against Cayce often have not studied his readings firsthand; therefore, they commit some fairly serious inaccuracies in their representation of them. On the other hand, the Cayce enthusiasts who defend him against the objections raised in certain Christian quarters often overlook what many Christians believe to be core or "fundamental" aspects of Christian faith when they attempt to show Cayce's compatibility with Christianity and the Bible. As one who is firmly committed to Christian faith but who is also convinced of the helpfulness of the Edgar Cayce readings, I have often wished that there were a publication that addressed these issues from a position that is sympathetic to *both* the Cayce readings *and* the more "fundamental" aspects of traditional Christian faith. After fifteen years of work with the readings and countless discussions with people from both "sides" of the controversy, I have decided the time has come to share what I have found in my own study of the readings and the Bible, for this study has been consistently an experience in discovering compatibility rather than conflict.

The purpose of this book, therefore, is to demonstrate that involvement with the work of Edgar Cayce and commitment to certain core Christian beliefs need not be mutually exclusive. I would emphasize that my objective is not to prove that either tradition is "right," nor to assert that Christianity is the *single* creed endorsed by the readings, but to show that one can affirm both Christianity and the Cayce material without being inconsistent in his or her beliefs.

Now, some students of the Cayce readings may question the appropriateness of such an effort, pointing out that the readings themselves discouraged us from arguing with those who would call this material anti-Christian. For example, when Edgar Cayce was once asked about how to respond to opposition from within the church, his response centered around such sentiments as,

" . . . do not cram them [the readings] down anyone's throat! Neither argue with them! Did thy Master ever argue, even when there were the greater railings or abuses?" (Edgar Cayce reading 262-61)

Yet is a reasoned response the same thing as cramming one's beliefs down another person's throat? I think not. While it is fruitless and even counterproductive to engage in arguments with those who are convinced that Edgar Cayce's readings are damaging to Christian faith, there is a place, I believe, for the nonargumentative exchange of thought. There are answers that can be made to many of the objections raised by some Christians, and merely to ignore the objections amounts to tacit agreement that there *are* no answers. For several reasons, I believe it is important that answers at least be offered wherever possible.

From the letters that come in to the A.R.E. on a regular basis and from conversations I have had with numerous people all over the United States and Canada, I know that there is a sizable group of people who are honestly seeking a reconciliation of the Cayce readings with their Christian faith. In many cases, these are people who might be helped by the readings and yet are troubled by the questions sometimes raised within their churches or by well-meaning friends and relatives. It is primarily for people in this position that I have written *Edgar Cayce and Christian Faith.* My hope is that the information to come will be a help to them in thinking through the issues at stake and in making their own decisions concerning the appropriateness of the Cayce information as part of their Christian worldview.

There is a second reason that I feel we have a responsibility to respond to Christian objections wherever possible. As general interest in Edgar Cayce grows and as A.R.E. membership multiplies, there is an increasingly large number of people who, though they have no personal conflict with the readings of Edgar Cayce, are drawn into debates with concerned Christian friends and family members. These members and friends of the A.R.E. may never have an affiliation with the traditional Christian church, yet the issues addressed here nonetheless touch them through their families and social relationships. For this segment of my readership, I hope that the material to follow clarifies the issues in such a way that future discussions with their more doctrinally conservative Christian friends and family members are characterized by greater understanding on both sides.

Finally, I suspect that among those who are speaking out against Edgar Cayce there are some who have relied upon secondhand information in forming their understanding of what his readings state. It's just possible that a certain number of people who think Edgar Cayce's work is anti-Christian would not think so if they were better acquainted with what his readings actually say. I hope that the information in this book will at least correct some common misconceptions concerning the content of the Cayce readings. My aim is not to "convert" Christians to enthusiasm for Edgar Cayce, but to encourage them to reconsider the opinion that others' enthusiasm must be seen as wrong.

I have titled this book *Edgar Cayce and Christian Faith* to emphasize the personal faith aspect of Christian belief, rather than affiliation with any particular version of the Christian religion. However, there *are* certain segments within the broader spectrum of Christian denominations from which objections to the work of Edgar Cayce most often arise. These are usually those denominations that place strong emphasis on the centrality of the redemptive work of Christ—or salvation through faith in Jesus—and reliance on the Bible as the final authority on all matters of doctrine. Of course, there are many labels that delineate the fine distinctions among the various lines of Christian belief. When I address myself to the questions often raised by Christians who describe themselves alternately as "fundamental," "Evangelical," "conservative," "charismatic," or "biblical," I do not mean to imply that these Christians speak for all of Christianity. Indeed, such branches are often described as being *outside* mainstream Christianity. Nevertheless, because it is from these quarters that objection is most frequently raised, I will focus on reconciling these more doctrinally conservative forms of Christianity with the Cayce readings.

Nor do I mean to imply that there are no differences of belief or distinctions of emphasis among those who go by such labels as "fundamental," "Evangelical," "conservative," "charismatic," or "biblical" Christian. Even among those who would join themselves under a single one of these labels, it would not be unusual to find differences on minor aspects of belief. Yet, I think it is accurate and fair to proceed on the assumption that these branches of Christianity do tend to hold positions in common concerning things psychic and the philosophy of reincarnation. It is to these common positions on such key issues that I address myself.

Edgar Cayce and Christian Faith is not intended to be a scholarly, theological work. It is written by a layperson for the layperson. While I have drawn on my background of college-level Bible study at a conservative Christian school, the reader will find the language and style of this book to be that of a popular, rather than an academic, work. I have started in Part One with a discussion of my own experience in integrating Cayce with Christian faith and then proceeded in Parts Two through Five to explore what seem to be the key issues in considering Edgar Cayce in the light of biblical Christianity.

Most readers will find it important to read the chapters of this book in the order in which they appear, as the book has been structured in such a way that each chapter builds on the preceding ones. The responses I offer in answer to Christian objections are not complicated, but still they often depend on the systematic building of one point upon another. It is not possible to discuss Edgar Cayce's appropriateness for Bible-believing Christians, for example, without first addressing the general field of psychic experience as it is approached in the Bible. Nor is it possible to address reincarnation and Christianity with a cookbook approach that mixes one part Bible verse with two parts Cayce readings. Instead, it is necessary to build an understanding of the key concepts underlying both reincarnation and a traditional Christian faith that emphasizes the salvific role of Christ, and then explore the compatibility of the two.

The questions raised and the answers proposed in the chapters to follow certainly do not cover every facet of either the Cayce readings or Christianity. I believe I have, however, dealt with the primary issues which must be resolved if one is to reconcile the Cayce readings with fundamental or core aspects of traditional Christian faith. I share my own approach to resolving these issues in the hope that it will help bridge the gap between two worlds that need not be separate.

For what was the judgement, what *is* judgement, what will ever be the judgement? They that deny that He hath come in the flesh are not worthy of acceptation. They that give thee that which is not helpful, hopeful, and patient and humble, and not condemning any, are not worthy!

This is thy judgement.

What, then, will you do with Jesus?

For He is the Way, He is the Light, He is the Hope, He *is* ready. Will you let Him into thy heart? or will you keep Him afar or apart? Will ye not eat of His body, of the bread of life? Drink from that fountain that He builds in the minds, the hearts, the souls of those that seek to know Him and His purposes with men, with the world!

Edgar Cayce reading 254-95

Part
One

How I Found Harmony Between
Edgar Cayce and Basic Christian Faith

1

A Personal Testimony

IT WAS WITH some hesitation that I chose to begin my discussion of *Edgar Cayce and Christian Faith* with a personal testimony. It seemed presumptuous to think that people would want to read my story. Maybe if I were famous there would be reason to consider my own experiences worth sharing. Or maybe if something astounding had happened to me I could justify taking up the time and pages that my story will fill. But merely to tell the story of how one ordinary person found harmony between the psychic work of Edgar Cayce and the tenets of Christianity did not seem momentous enough to launch a book.

Yet try as I would to begin my discussion in other ways, something was always lacking. I came to realize that it was important to begin with my story, not because people wanted to read about me, but because the *process* that I went through in integrating Edgar Cayce's readings with my Christianity is a process that countless other people are struggling with, have struggled with, or will struggle with. The Cayce readings advise us time and time again to speak from personal experience. We can share only that which we have lived. If my personal account helps any of my readers to recognize similar issues in their own spiritual lives, then the conceptual arguments developed in the subsequent parts of this book will have meaning. For theory that does not have a direct link to personal experience does have a way of ringing hollow in matters of religious faith.

There is another reason that I have chosen to share my personal testimony. I know that many Christians who acknowledge the Bible as the final authority in matters of faith believe it is impossible to be a Christian in their sense of the word and still be involved in the work of a psychic like Edgar Cayce. Similarly they would consider personal faith in Christ as the way to salvation as incompatible with the spiritual philosophy in the Cayce readings. I could tell them that I was a Christian and I'm not sure they would believe it. My hope is that in reading what in some Christian circles would be called "my testimony for Christ," my more fundamental readers will see that it is truly possible for one to remain rooted in Christian faith while believing in the work of Edgar Cayce. If involvement with Cayce is seen as an aberration in Christian faith (as it most surely *is* seen in some Christian circles), then I invite my Christian readers to follow my story closely and look for the place where I turned away from Christ in order to find Edgar Cayce. I don't think they will find such a circumstance.

Similarly, I hope that my story will in some way make the position of the doctrinally conservative Christian more understandable to the Edgar Cayce enthusiast who may be of a more liberal Christian persuasion, or no Christian persuasion at all. My purpose in writing this book is not to turn all Edgar Cayce enthusiasts into conservative Christians, nor to turn conservative Christians into Cayce enthusiasts. My purpose *is*, however, to attempt to show to each side the validity in the other side's position. Because the position of the doctrinally conservative Christian is such an uncompromising one, I know that some A.R.E. members consider it arbitrary and unreasonable. If in reading my story they catch some glimpse of the deep meaning behind this basic Christian faith, then I will feel that I have performed a worthwhile service.

Born Again in Jesus

I was only nine years old when I first came to know Jesus. And although childhood conversions are sometimes discounted because they are abandoned later on in life, I know that my faith in Christ could not have had any more real or sustained an effect on my life had it begun when I was an adult. It is still with a sense of wonder that I remember the night the Lord first called to me. I was lying on my bed, with nothing in particular on my mind, just looking at the pictures on my wallpaper. Suddenly I had an overwhelming desire to go to Sunday school.

Now I was not from a church-going family. I had the good fortune to come into this life with two good and loving parents, one of whom is a Christian and one of whom is an agnostic, but formal religious training was not a part of my early childhood. Our small town did not have a church of my mother's denomination, or I suppose my brother and I would have been raised in the tradition of that church. As it was, we had sporadically attended the little Baptist church in the neighborhood. At the time when the desire to attend Sunday school descended upon me, it had been several years since I had last been involved in any of that church's programs.

Suddenly I remembered with longing the Sunday school books filled with stories and pictures and cutouts of Bible characters. I just had to get one of those books! When a rummage through all the likely places failed to turn up any of my old Sunday school books, I knew I would have to overcome my natural shyness and once again attend the little Baptist Sunday school on the next block. That was no easy resolution to make. There had been a change of pastors and a change of most of the congregation since I had last been there, and I knew I would be walking into a room full of strangers. I also knew from past experience that when they spotted me out there in the congregation, they would make me stand up and give my name and tell everyone where I was from. Only the burning desire to see and hear those Bible stories made it possible for me to summon up my courage and walk into that church basement the next Sunday morning.

I was not disappointed. They *did* put me through the humiliating experience of standing up and saying who I was, but it was worth it. Some need in me was answered by the singing, the Bible drills, and the Bible lessons that came when we assembled in our classes. It wasn't long before I was firmly ensconced in not only the Sunday school but also the Friday night club for children. It was there, at "Awana Club," a month or two later that I met the Jesus who had called to me that night as I stared at my wallpaper. The minister's wife, who conducted the club meetings, was using the flannel board to explain the difference between believing *about* Jesus and having

Him in your heart. I realized that I'd always believed what the Bible says about Jesus. My mother had told me that Jesus was God, and about His resurrection and various other aspects of His life. Since I had been coming to Sunday school, I had certainly heard about His dying for our sins. I believed it all. But as I listened to the lesson that night, I understood for the first time what it meant to "ask Jesus into your heart." I knew I wanted that, and so as the closing prayer was prayed that night, I asked Him to come into my heart. It was a quiet and private event. No tears at an altar and no public testimonies. But I felt Jesus come in nonetheless. At the time, I hardly realized that I had set a direction for my entire life.

Growing in the Knowledge of Scripture

It was about this time that my father, himself an agnostic, bought me my first Bible. I had been "saving up" my Sunday school attendance to get one—after attending for a certain number of Sundays in a row, children were presented with their own Bibles in this Sunday school. But one evening even before I had earned my Sunday school Bible, I pulled my chair away from the table to sit down for supper and there on the seat was a plain, blue box. In it lay a beautiful, leather-bound King James Bible. It was printed on rice paper and the page edges were gilded. Not a child's Bible like I would have received at Sunday school, but the "real thing"!

Even though I stumbled over the unusual wording, and my patient mother spent many an hour "translating" the biblical text for me so that I could do my Sunday school homework and learn my Bible verses, my new Bible was a prized possession. Soon I could read it reasonably well by myself. My involvement with Sunday school eventually expanded to include church as well. The minister was giving a systematic series of sermons on the Book of Hebrews when I first began attending church. This circumstance is particularly interesting to me as I look back, because in my adult life the Book of Hebrews has been my favorite portion of Scripture. Both my love for and understanding of the Bible grew through those childhood years at the First Baptist Church. Shortly before my twelfth birthday, I was baptized and joined the church.

2

Exploring the Dimensions
of Biblical Faith

FROM THE BEGINNING, my involvement with the church and Christian life came from an inner motivation. I could sense that both my parents were pleased with this development in my life, but there was no specific urging from them that I continue. My beliefs were my own and they remained essentially private. Except for a few short ventures into the practice of "witnessing" to my older brother, I found it mildly embarrassing to openly discuss my faith. I think this feeling is common to many people. Yet as I entered my teen years, my sense that Jesus walked with me daily, heard my prayers, and spoke to me through the Scriptures quietly grew within me to the point where it became my primary interest in life. Paradoxically, the very intensity of my relationship with Jesus led me to explore what He might have to teach me outside of the church.

Striking Out on My Own

There had been a change in pastors since I had first joined the church, and the new minister brought a different perspective to the pulpit from the one I was accustomed to. It seems that the message of Christianity can stress joy and reconciliation with the Father through Christ, or it can stress fear and separation from the Father through sin. The new minister tended toward the latter approach. I became aware that I was seen as the child who came from a family of "unbelievers," and this made me uncomfortable. More and more came the unpleasant awareness that I was not in total agreement with this particular minister's perspective on life. At first I felt guilty about my differences of opinion over little matters, such as whether a Christian could enjoy Beatle music and not sin in the process. And then one day it dawned on me: If the Bible was truly God's revelation to humankind (which I believed with all my heart), then God could and would guide me in my understanding of it, just as surely as He guided the pastor.

I decided then and there to take a sabbatical from the church, not as a rejection of its teachings, but to let God speak to *me* through the Bible without the confusing guilt I'd been feeling over such petty private disagreements with the pastor. If I did that, then I would be sure that my beliefs were founded on my own relationship with the Lord and not on indoctrination. I was thirteen years old at the time and fairly sure that the people at church would not understand the reasons behind my decision, nor would they see the fine distinction between taking a sabbatical from church and rejecting Christian faith. They'd chalk my departure up to teenage rebellion, I thought, and so I just quietly dropped out of the picture. Oddly enough, no one ever asked why.

My Personal Search

I was very excited about this exploration of my faith. While I had had an active prayer life ever since I became a fundamental Christian, my private devotional life took on a new dimension now that I was "on my own." Since I did not have church and Sunday school to attend, the responsibility was on me to get the kind of nurturance and instruction that they had provided. I began having "church services" of my own. These later served as the prototype for my adult inner life. I also began studying in earnest.

My search led me to Bible history books and commentaries, some philosophy, and some works on world religions. But mostly I studied the Bible itself, relying on a concordance to do what I later learned in college were "word studies," taking particular words in the Bible, such as *faith* and *kingdom of God,* and studying them in every biblical context in which they appeared. I began to keep a notebook to record my word studies as well as highlights from my other reading. I found my convictions concerning the "fundamentals" of Christianity to deepen as my grounding in Scripture increased. It was a very special time in my spiritual life. In the meantime, high school with all of its peculiar traumas and challenges was happening in my life, and I was often glad to have the anchor of my faith to hold me during those years that are tempestuous for so many teenagers!

My First Encounter with Edgar Cayce

Prophecy was a particular interest of mine during those years. I had tried to sort it all out, studying the books of Daniel and Revelation, and making special studies of the Messianic prophecies. Once again, I read a few outside sources, such as the prophecies of Nostradamus, but for the most part my studies were confined to what I could read in the Bible and a basic Bible handbook. I had long ago developed the habit of praying for guidance as I studied the Bible, and that seemed to work pretty well.

When we were given the option of choosing any subject for a high school English research paper, I was ready to jump into prophecy with both feet. But, of course, part of the point of the assignment was to teach basic research skills, and so I was obliged to expand my horizons a bit and research some literature besides the Bible on the subject of prophecy. That is when I happened upon my first Edgar Cayce book, *Edgar Cayce on Prophecy*. (Paperback Library, Inc., N.Y., 1968) Strangely enough, this book did not seem the least bit odd or unusual to me as I read through it. It fascinated me, because it seemed that the prophecies of this man called Edgar Cayce wove in and out of the biblical tapestry in such a way as to complement and harmonize with what I had already read in the Bible. But I felt the need for caution, too, as I always did when considering new material in my studies, and I turned to prayer and my Bible for guidance concerning this new and unusual source of information.

What I found when I opened my Bible at random[1] was this passage:

> Beloved, believe not every spirit, but try the spirits whether they are of God: because many false

prophets are gone out into the world. Hereby know ye the Spirit of God: Every spirit that confesseth that Jesus Christ is come in the flesh is of God: And every spirit that confesseth not that Jesus Christ is come in the flesh is not of God . . . I John 4:1-3a

I was sure that *Edgar Cayce on Prophecy* had included some quotes from Cayce about Jesus Christ coming in the flesh, but I went back and checked anyway. There it was, among the other Cayce prophecies being discussed on page 28: "The Lord, then, will come, 'even as ye have seen him go.'" (262-49)

Then, later on in the book, where Edgar Cayce's general approach to spiritual development was being explained, this reading was quoted: "He asked, 'Whom say men that I am?' Then Peter answered, 'Thou art the Christ, the son of the living God!' Then, 'Upon this I will build my church, and the gates of hell shall not prevail against it.'" (262-87)

It seemed clear to me that these readings affirmed the centrality of Christ. They even stressed His second coming as part of the prophecies of our day. For the time being, I was satisfied. I included some Edgar Cayce information in my research paper on prophecy, thought he sounded like an interesting person, and didn't really think about him again for six months.

Questions and More Questions

Nearly three years had passed since I'd begun my private search, and now new issues were clamoring for attention in my Bible studies. Firmly rooted in my belief in salvation by faith in Jesus, I still had some questions that puzzled and troubled me. I had begun to worry about the people who were going to hell because they did not believe in Jesus. I prayed for the ones who were my acquaintances and even talked to a few people about Jesus, but continued to be troubled by what looked to me like a stacked deck. Did all people *really* have equal access to Jesus and the grace He offers? If not, then something did not fit together in the doctrine that nonbelievers would go to hell.

It had been explained to me when I was still in Sunday school that this teaching only applied to the people who had had the opportunity to hear about Jesus but rejected Him. The others, who died truly in ignorance of His atonement, would be judged according to how they lived up to their consciences. But this answer still did not quite solve the problem. Even given a chance to hear the Gospel, didn't some people's circumstances predispose them to accept it while others' circumstances conditioned them to reject it?

This was not just hypothetical thinking on my part. My dearest friend was a Jewish girl whose family was committed to their heritage. Since childhood, she had been on my prayer list, and once or twice I had even made an awkward attempt to tell her about my faith. But did my friend really have the same opportunity to accept Jesus that I had had? It had been relatively easy for me, what with parental approval and a church on the next block that I could walk to. I imagined it was even easier, more "natural" for a child in a church-going family to accept Christ. Certainly a decision for Christ was more personal than just a family affiliation with a church, but even taking that into account, weren't the odds just a bit more against my friend than they had been for me? To put it succinctly, under the doctrine that only those who accept Jesus will be "saved," doesn't the minister's son stand a greater chance of being "saved" than a rabbi's son? I did not have to go so far as to consider the people in Africa, who've never heard of Jesus, to see that all did not have quite the same opportunity to believe.

Next came the questions about birth defects and the poverty-stricken and the oppressed. In response to the apparent unfairness in life, the fundamentalist Christian position usually was that people who had suffered hardships like these on earth would have it made up to them in heaven. This hardly seemed to even out the inequities. My faith promised me that I would go to heaven, too—and I was having a rather easy and pleasant life here on earth, to boot. Didn't I still come out with a better deal than those who suffered in this life and later went to heaven?

Worse yet, what of those who were dealt a bad hand in this life and who also chose not to accept Jesus? Not only would they be denied heaven, but they would also have spent their earthly lives with hardship or handicap or whatever unfortunate circumstances may have come their way. The person who happened into pleasant life circumstances or a sound body, yet failed to accept Christ, might end up going to hell, but at least he or she had had a decent life here on earth. There was just no way that I could see the afterlife as an adequate equalizer of life's inequities.

These questions did not put God on trial in my mind. My personal faith remained in Jesus, and I could not imagine my own life without that living relationship. Yet I could not deny the feeling that something was missing in the traditional explanations for my questions. I searched my Bible and prayed for guidance.

3

Discovering Edgar Cayce

EVEN THOUGH I had encountered Edgar Cayce in the
course of my research on prophecy, it was not until six
months later that I really "discovered" his work. My interest in prophecy had eventually led to a more general
interest in things psychic, and I had begun to add some
study of parapsychology to my reading. Some of what I
read about the psychic field seemed to parallel closely
what I had felt and experienced in my own Christian inner life. Other aspects felt foreign and inappropriate for
me. I began to consult the Bible concerning psychic experiences and found that they certainly were mentioned. I also found that definite guidelines were given

in Scripture regarding the use of psi. It is on the basis of those guidelines that I have developed the material that comprises Part Two of this book, "Psychic Experience and Contemporary Christianity." Leaving an in-depth discussion of those guidelines for later, let me mention at this point that I found within my Bible enough instruction on psychic experience to form what I believed was a biblically based approach to the field.

My reading soon led me to my second Edgar Cayce book, *The World Within.* This work, which deals with the Edgar Cayce readings on reincarnation, not only introduced me to the topics of reincarnation and karma, but also kindled my first real interest in the story of this remarkable psychic. As I read *The World Within,* my excitement steadily mounted, for here were the answers I had been looking for. Here were the explanations of the apparent inequities in life. And here was the most complete explanation I had ever come across of why life is the way it is.

Now if my readers of Bible-based Christian persuasion did not part company with me when I began to talk about a biblically based approach to psi, here is probably where the alarm bells are really going off. For the concept of reincarnation is usually seen as the most dangerous and anti-Christian heresy into which one could be led. I will not go into the substance of my response to that charge here, for it comprises all of Part Four of this book. Instead, I ask those who view reincarnation as incompatible with the saving work of Jesus Christ to suspend temporarily their theological objections to reincarnation and for now simply consider the *steps* through which I became involved with it and the work of Edgar Cayce.

For me, the concept of reincarnation did not cancel out the truth of Christian faith. It certainly did not weaken my personal faith *and my trust in Christ as the way of salvation.* What it did do, however, was put together the loose ends in my belief system. It made me realize that we really do have free will in this life and that each one of us is responsible for doing the very best we can with the circumstances that come to us. For if there was a central message for me in the reincarnation concept, it was that all circumstances come to us for our own growth and good. That was the greatest piece of practical advice I'd ever received!

The helpfulness of this Cayce book on reincarnation made me want to find out everything I could concerning the work of this man. I began to search for the biography, *There Is a River,* that had been mentioned in *The World Within.* I went to the public library, the school library, and a couple of bookstores. I came up blank. But I was apparently meant to read that Cayce biography, for "happenstance" (better known as "synchronicity") intervened.

One day my mother happened to take a walk to the grocery store (she usually drove) right around the time when I was searching for the Cayce biography, and she ran into a neighbor whose habit was to walk to the store. They had not seen each other to converse in years, but that day their spontaneous meeting led to an extended conversation. I still don't know exactly how the casual exchange got from "How is your daughter?" to a mention of the kind of books I was reading, but that's just what happened. The neighbor said she had some books she thought might interest me, and the next day stopped by with a grocery bag full. *There Is a River* was right on top!

For me, as for so many others, reading that book was one of the most enthralling experiences of my life. While it is a very subjective evaluation to say, "It rang true for me," that is just what it did. It's not that my biblical faith was inadequate or faltering, but that this information dovetailed with it, making me see new ways that God was at work in the world and through those people who are willing to be His instruments. I can honestly say that it did not lead me away from my faith or to a new faith, but that it deepened and confirmed the faith I already had.

That is not to say that I jumped headlong into Cayce without another thought that his work might not be in line with God's revelation through the Bible. I had been steeped too long in a conservative approach that took the Bible's warnings about false prophets seriously to overlook the possibility that the Cayce material might be false teaching. I returned once again to the Bible's warnings concerning false prophets and did a lot of praying as I studied them. I measured the information in Edgar Cayce's readings against every biblical standard I could and found it to be in keeping with the Bible's teaching.

How can this be when so many fundamental Christian writers have "exposed" Cayce's alleged departures from biblical doctrine? My only response at this juncture is to suggest that perhaps those writers have not examined the Cayce material as closely as they might have. As I hope to demonstrate in the remaining parts of this book, there is no teaching in the Edgar Cayce readings that violates a fundamental article of Christian faith. Particularly in Part Three we will look at many of the Christian doctrines that Cayce is accused of subverting and see whether this is really the case. Then, as mentioned before, Part Four will address the issue of whether or not reincarnation is compatible with a Christian faith in Jesus Christ. In the meantime, I will approach these questions from the perspective of my own experience as it unfolded at that time.

By the time I had finished reading *There Is a River,* I knew that more than anything else I wanted to be directly involved with the work of Edgar Cayce some day.

My edition of the biography did not contain any current information about the organization Cayce founded, so I wrote a somewhat blind letter to the Edgar Cayce Foundation, Virginia Beach, Virginia (no street address or zip code) asking, in essence, "Are you still there, and if so can I join?" When my response came, it turned out that the organization had a network of small groups in cities and towns all over the world. The network was called the Search for God® Study Group Program, and it featured small groups meeting informally in private homes to discuss concepts from the Edgar Cayce readings. There was a group that met not more than twenty minutes from my home.

I was enthusiastic over the prospect of joining such a group. I read and reread the brochure I'd been sent, which described the format of a meeting and told how in some areas a number of study groups organized to form "councils" that could carry on larger meetings and activities at the local level. I was by now gung-ho and I knew it. Before I made the step of contacting the group, I decided to ask one more time whether I should become involved in "the Work," as I'd read Edgar Cayce had called it. The gist of my prayer for guidance was, "Lord, You know that I am really drawn to this work. All of the guidance I've received so far seems to have told me it's right to become involved with it. But I know that we can be led astray, and I don't want to go down the wrong track. If this work is wrong, *please* show me now." I opened my Bible at random, and this is what awaited me when I opened my eyes and looked at the page:

> . . . if this counsel or this work be of men, it will come to nought: But if it be of God, ye cannot over-throw it; lest haply ye be found even to fight against God. Acts 5:38b-39

I went to my first A.R.E. study group meeting. From the first, I felt at home there. These people were not kooks or psychic dabblers, but people just like myself who were seeking to grow in their relationship with God. My host and hostess were unquestionably Christians, active in their church and committed to their faith. For years their home had been a place where others, who came because of an interest in Edgar Cayce, found a similar faith. My study group soon became a spiritual family and our group meetings the highlight of my week. For at each meeting we not only discussed concepts from the Bible and the Edgar Cayce readings, but we also grappled with helping each other live those concepts in our daily lives each week between the meetings. As is typical at an A.R.E. study group, each meeting closed with a period of group meditation and prayer—prayer in the name of Christ for one another, for our loved ones, for those who had requested our prayers. The meditation experience was new to me, but I soon learned this delightfully simple practice of being quiet long enough to wait on the presence of the Lord.

4

The Baptism of the Holy Spirit

DURING THIS PERIOD when my involvement with the A.R.E. was growing, my involvement with the church took on new life as well. A lady in town, who knew I was very interested in religion but had no church affiliation, invited me to a service at her Assembly of God, which is Pentecostal or charismatic in its form of worship. At this time, the charismatic movement had really begun to take hold in the United States and more and more Christians from all denominations were experiencing what they called the Baptism of the Holy Spirit. Based on New Testament accounts of believers being "baptized in the Holy Ghost" and speaking in tongues, this Pentecostal movement preaches that such experiences are available to Christians today.

My Introduction to Pentecostalism

I knew very little about Pentecostalism before I attended my first service, my only source of information being some of the derogatory remarks sometimes made about so-called "holy rollers." Yet as soon as I entered that church and the service was under way, I knew that the Spirit of God was alive and well in that congregation. Here, finally, was a church that did not believe the Spirit stopped manifesting in the world as soon as the last page of the New Testament was complete. These people took seriously the idea that the gifts of the Holy Spirit were not confined to the early church but can be a vital part of the church today. The way they prayed, the way they sang, the way they worshiped was a testimony to that vitality. One could not help but feel spiritually alive in that church. Here was another part of what I had been looking for.

The sermon that evening was about the Baptism of the Holy Spirit. The minister talked about Jesus' promise concerning the Spirit, as reported in John's Gospel:

> If any man thirst, let him come unto me, and drink. He that believeth on me, as the scripture hath said, out of his belly shall flow rivers of living water. (But this spake he of the Spirit, which they that believe on him should receive: for the Holy Ghost was not yet given; because that Jesus was not yet glorified.) John 7:37b-39

The sermon went on to include the story of Pentecost and the outpouring of the Holy Spirit that came on that day. The preacher pointed out subsequent New Testament reports of believers being baptized in the Holy Spirit and speaking in tongues. He called the congregation's attention to numerous passages which indicate that the church of New Testament times practiced the gifts of the Holy Spirit. Finally, he invited those in the congregation who had not received the Baptism of the Holy Spirit to come forward if they wished to do so.

There was no hesitation in my mind as I walked to the front of the church that night. The scriptural ground seemed firm for the Baptism of the Holy Spirit. The concept that " . . . we know not what we should pray for as we ought: but the Spirit itself maketh intercession for us with groanings which cannot be uttered" (Romans 8:26) hit home for me. How many times in meditation had I felt something that could not be formed into a prayer in the English language? I knew from my own experience that religion must be both intellectual and "emotional," rational and nonrational. In the light of more recent right-brain/left-brain research, I have come to understand this in terms of recognizing the difference between the rational, logical thought processes of the left brain and the oft-denied intuitive and nonrational function of the right brain. It seems that both aspects of consciousness must be important to spiritual life. Language is the ultimate expression of the rational, logical left-brain function. What better outlet for the Spirit flowing within than the ecstatic speaking in an unknown tongue?

Experiencing the Baptism

As the elders of the church laid hands on me to pray, I could not help but notice a striking concurrence with what I'd learned about prayer for healing in my A.R.E. experience. One elder placed his hands so that he lightly held my head back to front, one palm on my forehead, one palm at the base of my skull. The other elder placed his palms on either side of my head, one hand just above each ear.

Now as I'd worked with and studied the theories behind meditation, I had learned that, according to the Edgar Cayce readings and several other Eastern and mystical sources, there are so-called "spiritual centers" within each of us, sort of meeting places where the soul connects with the body. These are not physical structures, but they are said to correspond with the major endocrine gland centers of the body. The elders had placed their hands so as to surround the two highest spiritual centers, those associated with the pituitary and the pineal glands. This is exactly what I had seen done at A.R.E. prayer-for-healing sessions.

As the elders began to pray for me, I prayed, too, asking for, acknowledging, and accepting the Baptism of the Holy Spirit. A tremendous light began to glow and then swell inside of me, deep in my abdominal cavity. It grew and began to rise in a column, like a spring emerging from the earth. By now the elders were praying in tongues. Suddenly the light exploded in my head, and I felt my whole body bathed in a golden light. I was praying in tongues. Not hesitantly or shyly, as I had expected to do, but fervently and ecstatically, the tears of absolute joy running down my face. I had had a classic "kundalini" experience.

The kundalini experience, as students of the Edgar Cayce readings will know, is related to those spiritual centers just mentioned. There is an ancient belief that these centers conduct spiritual energy through the body, much the same way that wiring will conduct electricity through your home. In Eastern traditions this force is called the "kundalini" force. The practice of prayer and meditation will activate and circulate this energy, which tends to move upward through the body during times of spiritual attunement. The ultimate, or "peak," spiritual experience is to have this kundalini energy move all the way up to the two highest centers of the body (those associated with the pituitary and pineal glands), from which point it will cascade downward throughout the body in a healing, glowing light.

In all of my work with meditation, I had never experienced this ultimate movement of the light. That night, as I received the Baptism of the Holy Spirit, it happened.

That night I went home and read again all of the Scripture passages that the minister had used in his sermon. In the eyes of many Christians, this Baptism of the Holy Spirit and the speaking in tongues was outside the mainstream, a bit on the fringes, even. It had all seemed scripturally sound to me, and my experience had been confirming. Still, I followed my custom of asking God to show me if any new idea or experience to which I was drawn was erroneous. I prayed that He would let me know whether I was right in accepting this new dimension to Christian life.

That night I dreamed of the grammar school I had attended in childhood. In my dream, I was leaving my kindergarten classroom. As I left the room and walked out of the school, I crossed the street to the playground, where in real life there sits a large, stone drinking fountain that had been dry for as long as I could remember. In my dream, I walked up to that fountain, turned the handle, and took a long, refreshing drink. "He that believeth on me . . . out of his belly shall flow rivers of living water." (John 7:38) When I awakened, I knew the Lord had answered my prayer for guidance.

Bridging the Gap

My involvement with that Assembly of God was a

source of great joy. For the first time since my departure from the Baptist church four years before, I was again part of a formal church and Sunday school. I found that, side by side with my A.R.E. study group involvement, this new church life made my sense of affiliation with the Christian community complete. I realized that I'd been missing the nurturance of a church involvement.

But my newfound affiliation was not without its challenges. I was now in regular contact with people who believed Edgar Cayce's work was of the devil and who tried their best to show me the error of my ways. I certainly did not advertise my A.R.E. involvement, but neither did I hide it like a deep, dark secret. It was nothing to be ashamed of, and I did not want to treat it as such. I suppose my discussions with well-meaning Christian friends in that church were the beginnings of what I am laying out in this book today. For even then, it saddened (and often frustrated) me to see Edgar Cayce's wonderfully helpful work misunderstood and condemned. It became a sense of mission for me to show other people that the two worlds could be bridged, as I had bridged them myself.

My Baptism in the Spirit presented a particular problem for my Pentecostal friends. They believed I could not be a Christian and believe in reincarnation. They also believed that you could not receive the Baptism of the Holy Spirit unless you were first truly a Christian. I believed in reincarnation, and I had also received the Baptism of the Holy Spirit before their very eyes. *That* was a problem!

Some people suggested that when I prayed for guidance on matters such as the work of Edgar Cayce and received confirmation, it was the devil and not God who had answered my prayers. What answer can there be to that? If I, as a Christian trusting in Christ and earnestly asking Him to guide me in matters of such eternal import, got answers from the devil instead, what hope is there for any of us?

I was told that the Bible, and not a subjective sense of right and wrong, was the only sure means of staying on the right track. Yet I *had* turned to my Bible every step of the way. It was in the Bible itself that I found each piece of confirmation. If my reading of the Bible leads me to a different understanding than yours does, does that make my reading subjective and yours objective? As long as we read the Bible in a way that is true to the context, who is to say that one reading is the right one and another is the wrong one?

On and on the questions and the debates went, my fundamental Christian friends sometimes arguing with me, sometimes praying for me, but always certain that I was bound for hell. Meanwhile, my sense of the Lord's presence grew; and, with that sense, that conviction that my beliefs were acceptable before Him also grew.

Being Willing to Make the Sacrifice

My exposure to the anti-Edgar Cayce line of thinking was not limited to these personal discussions with church friends. I had also begun to read the books that attempt to discredit Cayce and had gone to hear some well-known authors speak on the subject. One evening as I listened to a particularly gifted Christian writer and speaker expound on the dangers of "Cayceism," I asked myself, "Have I become too smug, too sure of the rightness of my beliefs?" I had reached the point where I felt quite able to counter every anti-Cayce argument I had ever heard, and suddenly it occurred to me: Unless you are able to give something up—*anything* you hold precious in your personal scheme of things—it will become your god. Was I willing to give up the A.R.E.? Surely I believed it was right, something that added to my spiritual life. But the A.R.E. was not meant to be a faith, the way Christianity is a faith. Had I made it one?

That night I went home and I struggled with this new challenge in front of me. I still could see nothing anti-Christian in the Cayce material; in fact, it seemed to be God-sent into my life; *but was I willing to give it up, if that was what God wanted me to do?* It wasn't easy, and there were many tears and regrets that night as I thought of all that had been dear to me in my A.R.E. involvement. But finally I reached the point where I could honestly pray, "Lord, I'm ready to leave all of this behind if that's what You want me to do." I fell asleep feeling at peace.

The next day was Sunday and so I went to church, wondering what the day held in store. That morning the pastor preached on the story of Abraham's near-sacrifice of Isaac. Abraham had prayed for a son, been promised a son by God; and finally in Abraham's old age, God had given him Isaac. For Abraham, Isaac represented all that God had ever promised him. Now God was asking Abraham to sacrifice Isaac. How could this be? How could God be asking Abraham to sacrifice the very thing that had been God's own gift to him? Yet that was what God asked of Abraham, and finally Abraham came to the point where he was ready to obey. That was all it took. Once Abraham was truly ready to sacrifice Isaac, the son that he loved, God interceded and told him the sacrifice was not necessary. The point of this requested sacrifice, the minister pointed out, was to be certain that Abraham still worshiped and obeyed God, rather than the form that God's promise had taken. Once Abraham had demonstrated that his primary allegiance and obedience were still with God, the sacrifice was no longer necessary.

I left church that morning with a lump in my throat and a gratitude in my heart that was indescribable. I, too, had been tested. I, too, had had to come to the point of being willing to sacrifice what I believed was a God-given gift. Like Abraham, I had been stopped at the moment when I was truly ready to obey and make the sacrifice. Never before or since have I felt closer to the love of God.

5

Making the Integration Complete

I BEGAN THIS book by expressing some hesitancy to start with my own story. That was some four chapters ago, and it's time now to go on to the substance of the theological integration that can be made between the readings of Edgar Cayce and the fundamentals, basics, or core beliefs of conservative Christianity. Only one chapter of my personal story remains to be told before I feel ready to present the evidence for this integration as I have found it in the Bible.

As the experiences I shared in the last chapter were taking place, my high school years were drawing to a close, and I faced the usual vocational decisions that come with that time of life. I knew that I wanted to work in the field of spiritual enlightenment, but that urge filled a rather amorphous space in my aspirations. I could not imagine what kind of job my interests suggested for me, let alone what kind of college training I should seek. I only knew that I wanted to study the Bible and religion. I decided to pursue that step first and let the career definition come later.

Finding a place to study the Bible was not as easy as I would have expected. I looked into a few church-affiliated schools that offered majors in religion or theology, but most of these were aligned with the more liberal branches of Protestantism, and I found that their orientation was more humanistic than what I was looking for. I wanted to study the Bible in a setting where it was seen as the infallible word of God, and where the supernatural and miraculous within its pages would be taken as fact rather than myth.

A short distance from where I grew up, there was a small, church-affiliated liberal arts/Bible college that had been founded as a missionary training institute. I knew very little about the denomination, but I did know that it was Evangelical in its leanings. I decided to find out more about the school's programs and philosophy, so I drove up one day and requested a copy of the college catalog.

Everything I read as I studied that catalog made me want to go to that school. The courses offered in-depth study of the Bible, Christian theology, and related religious issues. Not only that, but the school stressed the importance of a liberal arts education alongside the biblical training. Its founder was committed to the idea that Christians should not be ignorant when it came to literature, music, philosophy, and science. This was exactly what I had been looking for!

There was only one problem. This school *was* very

conservative in its outlook on Christian life. From the catalog and the application form, it was clear that the entrance requirements included not only an orthodoxy of faith, but the signing of a pledge not to smoke, dance, drink, or go to the movies while attending that school. The pledge was no problem. I was not inclined to the first three activities, and I rarely got out to the movies anyway. But the very existence of such a pledge made me realize that my A.R.E. involvement would be considered highly irregular!

I was still pretty sure I wanted to attend the school, but did wonder whether I would find it too restrictive. I decided the best approach was to leave it in God's hands. I would fill out my application, making no effort to hide my A.R.E. affiliation. If they accepted me to the school, knowing of my leanings, I would feel comfortable about going. If they rejected me on the basis of my belief in the Edgar Cayce readings, then I knew I would not have been happy at that school anyway. Either way, what was meant to happen, would happen. I submitted my application and waited.

A few weeks later, I was called by the admissions officer for an interview. Several of the deans and the college's vice-president were there when I arrived for my appointment. I later learned that such preadmission interviews were practically unheard of. Not surprisingly, they were concerned about the unorthodox activities my application had admitted to. They wanted to ask me about them in order to better determine my appropriateness as a student at their school.

Everyone was polite. They were not aggressive in their questioning, but it was clear that they considered the A.R.E. to be a subversive activity, for one of them asked me if I would try to form "cells" on campus if I were accepted to that school. I assured them that my aim was not to convert other Christians to Edgar Cayce and that I had no desire to stir things up on campus. I did want to share the message in Edgar Cayce's readings, but felt it was most appropriately shared with people who were looking for something, rather than those who had already found their faith. This seemed to satisfy the committee, and the outcome of that meeting was the tacit agreement that I could come to their college if I agreed not to spread my heresy among the students.

If I had my college years to do over again, I would again choose that school without hesitation. The quality of instruction was high, and the professors showed an impressive combination of Evangelical Christian faith and intellectual openness. I know that many people outside of this particular form of Christian persuasion feel that those two traits are mutually exclusive, but I saw much evidence to the contrary during my four years at that college. I graduated with a deepened respect for and commitment to basic Christian faith. I also remained convinced that my study of the Cayce readings only augmented that commitment.

My plan to take my vocational decisions one step at a time worked well, too, for within a year after graduation I "knew" it was time to move to Virginia Beach and study the Cayce readings with the same intensity with which I had studied the Bible during those college years. I had no job lined up, nor did I have a place to live, but I knew that if I was meant to be there, things would work out. Besides, I could always go back home if things did not work out in Virginia Beach. Secretly, I even hoped they would not work out, because I was happy at home and reluctant to leave. I gave myself a month to test the Virginia Beach "experiment."

The success of my experimental move exceeded anything I had dreamed of. I was offered a job the very day I arrived at Virginia Beach. Not just a job, but a JOB AT THE A.R.E.! Never did I expect something so wonderful as that to happen. It was only a part-time job as a receptionist and bookstore clerk, but I was thrilled to be actually working at a place that meant so much to me. Within a week I had also found a tiny house to live in, so incredibly inexpensive that I could swing it on my part-time pay. Never again did I doubt that I was meant to stay in Virginia Beach.

In the years since then, lots of good things have happened, both vocationally and personally. My life to this point has been an experience in realizing that God really is there to show us the truth if we will listen. The important thing is not to become so focused on what we expect or want to hear that the real message passes by us, unnoticed. "God moves in mysterious ways," the old saying goes, and I do not think this applies to anything in life more than it does to God's ways of leading or guiding us into truth. I'd like to illustrate this point, and use it to set the tone for all that is to follow in this book, by concluding here with this story:

During my years at college, I made relatively few friends among my fellow students. While I kept my promise not to "spread" the Edgar Cayce story among the students, I did not hide my involvement from those students I got to know socially. Usually the discovery of my "heresy" drastically changed the nature of a friendship, for once someone learned of it, he or she would devote the rest of our relationship to straightening me out. These Bible students were a committed lot!

But two friends stand out as exceptions to that pattern. They were a married couple who, though they could not accept my beliefs, respected them and did not try to change them. We occasionally discussed psychic and metaphysical concepts, but I tried to be careful not to push them. I wanted to show them the same live-and-let-live respect that they had shown me.

Then one time after we had all graduated and I had

moved to Virginia Beach I had a visit from this couple.
This time as we discussed matters spiritual and philosophical, I sensed a change. The husband seemed to be
questioning some of the things he had been very sure of
while in college. He was now asking me about Edgar
Cayce as if he really wanted the answers for personal reasons. I decided the time was right to make a more overt
gesture of invitation to explore the Cayce material, and
so I invited my friend to attend a lecture that was taking
place at A.R.E. that night. He accepted quite eagerly.

The topic that evening focused on Jesus, and the
speaker was one whom I knew to be especially gifted in
presenting the Edgar Cayce readings on that subject. He,
too, was from a Christian background and carried much
of that orientation into his work with the readings. As I
listened to him speak that night, I was nothing short of
awed to realize that every question my friend had raised
earlier that day was being addressed. I took a sideways
glance and saw that he was writing notes just as fast as
the lecturer spoke. The Spirit is moving, I thought! I listened carefully to each point of the lecture, trying to hear
it through the ears of a conservative Christian who was
hearing it for the first time. It fit beautifully with everything I knew my friend had learned at that Bible college.

When the talk was over, I could hardly wait to get my
friend's reaction. Already in my mind he was a new Edgar
Cayce enthusiast. I turned to him expectantly. He merely
shook his head slowly, saying, "Lynn, you're even further
off base than I thought you were!" That evening was a
lesson I'll never forget concerning the ultimate subjec-
tivity of our perceptions. We can all hear the same words,
yet each get his or her own understanding of them.

But more important than that lesson was the other
realization that came to me later that same evening. We
all went out for ice cream and had a discussion about
the lecture. As my friend attempted to refute, point by

point, each concept that had been presented in the lecture, I saw his own faith, the faith that had been faltering a few hours before, rekindle and grow strong. Had my purpose in inviting him to the lecture been to turn him into an Edgar Cayce enthusiast, or had it been to help him find new meaning in his faith? If my purpose was the former, it had failed, as well it should have. If my purpose was the latter, then it had been met, even though it didn't happen the way I'd expected it to.

So it is with the presentation coming on the following pages. I would like to think that everyone who reads my evidence will conclude that Edgar Cayce's readings are indeed compatible with biblical Christianity. Yet I know that will not be the case. We each must have our own understanding of truth; not that there is no ultimate Truth, but each of us must see the Truth as best we can from our own perspective. Like the proverbial blind men and the elephant, we can sometimes feel that our concept of truth is irreconcilable with that of another person.

If the arguments I present in the pages to come convince some people that Cayce and Christianity are compatible, if they make others wonder whether *maybe* they are compatible, and if they leave the rest only more firmly rooted in their faith as they conclude that the two are *not* compatible, I will be content.

Part
Two

Psychic Experience and
Contemporary Christianity

6

The Nature of Psychic Experience

BEFORE WE CAN ask whether Edgar Cayce's psychic readings are compatible with Christianity, we must address the broader question surrounding psychic experience as a whole. For there are two levels of objection to the Edgar Cayce material. One is based on the content of his readings. Objections of this sort arise from perceived violations of fundamental Christian doctrine in the concepts and philosophy that emerge from these readings. The most common of these objections will be addressed in Parts Three, Four, and Five.

But there is another, more basic, level of objection that arises from the conviction that all psychic information, regardless of its content, comes in direct violation of the Bible's teaching. It is essential that we examine this charge before going any further: If it is true that the Bible gives a blanket condemnation of all psychic experience, then the readings of Edgar Cayce cannot be defended using biblical criteria. If, on the other hand, we can make a case for the permissibility of psychic experience within certain guidelines, then we can go on to discuss whether the Cayce readings, as a specific instance of psychic experience, measure up to those guidelines.

The Science of Parapsychology

I will not attempt here to validate, justify, or "prove" the existence of psychic phenomena. For the purposes of this discussion, it is enough to acknowledge the growing popular interest in, and apparent experience with, psychic phenomena of all types. This widespread popularity alone, regardless of the scientific claims made for psychic research, is cause for concern among many Christians who believe such experiences are demonically inspired.

Certainly the field of psychic experience remains a controversial one for scientists of our day. Despite the acceptance of parapsychology by the American Academy for the Advancement of Science in the 1970s, and despite recurring reports during that same time that both the U.S. and Soviet governments were making serious inquiries into the question of the psychic potential of humans, the scientific validity of psychical research is still challenged by some of the great scientists and thinkers of our day. In recent years, the controversy over parapsychology has been kept well stirred by challenges from the Committee for the Scientific Investigation of Claims of the Paranormal (CSICOP), which boasts or has boasted among its most outspoken members such notables as the late science fiction writer Isaac Asimov and The Amazing Randi, the magician. The late Carl Sagan was also a prominent spokesperson for CSICOP. There would be little point in my attempting to add here to an argument that some of the greatest scientific minds of our day have failed to resolve.

Be that as it may, it is still appropriate to consider the implications of parapsychology, should it turn out to be scientifically valid. In the first place, most Christians who object to psychic phenomena do so not because they believe such phenomena do not occur, but because they believe they are occurring at the devil's instigation. There is just too much evidence of psychic experience in the Bible for Bible-believing Christians to deny its reality. In the second place, it is not too soon to be asking ourselves what the spiritual implications of parapsychological research may be, should it eventually be proved valid beyond a shadow of a doubt.

The Classes of Psychic Experience

The types of psychic experience are many, and it can sometimes be misleading to address the entire field of psychic phenomena as a unit. Many of the books which warn Christians of the dangers of psychic experience will group all paranormal phenomena, from telepathy to witches' spells, into one category. While it is true that paranormal phenomena hold the common characteristic of being inexplicable under natural law, the differences between the various types of phenomena can be great. It is worthwhile, then, to take time to sort out and categorize the different forms that paranormal phenomena can take.

The Varieties of ESP. Of course, the most basic and most often talked about psychic experience is extrasensory perception or ESP. Actually, this term does not designate one single phenomenon, but a whole category of psychic experiences that have to do with perception. ESP is, by the broadest definition of the term, perception without use of the five senses. The ability to acquire knowledge by some means other than the physical senses can take several forms.

If one receives extrasensory knowledge of an external object or event, the phenomenon is called "clairvoyance." Although this designation has the literal meaning of "clear seeing," the knowledge does not necessarily have to be relayed via visual imagery. If one were to "know" of something taking place outside the range of the senses, even though the event was not seen in the mind's eye, that would be clairvoyance. Closely related to clairvoyance is "clairaudience," which involves "hearing" things psychically rather than seeing them.

Telepathy involves communication from one mind to another without any physical medium or use of the five senses. The telepathic process typically involves both a "sender"—the one whose thoughts are being perceived—and a "receiver"—the one who psychically picks up the information. Although the main telepathic function seems to rest on the receiver, there is some evidence that the ability of the sender to transmit is also a factor in the telepathic communication.

A third type of ESP is precognition, the ability to know something before it happens. Retrocognition, the ability to psychically perceive something that has happened in the past, shares precognition's feature of transcending normal time consciousness. Both phenomena challenge the notion that time is real in an absolute sense and that the past, the present, and the future progress through that which we call time in a linear fashion.

Psychokinesis. A second major category of paranormal experience is psychokinesis, often abbreviated as "PK." This phenomenon is also sometimes called "telekinesis" or "mind over matter." PK may take the form of moving objects with the mind or causing things to happen in one's environment with the power of one's thoughts, but the main delineating characteristic of all psychokinetic phenomena is that there is direct mental influence over a physical object or an objective process.

Parapsychology and Psi. Extrasensory and psychokinetic phenomena, taken as a whole, are sometimes described by the word *psi* taken from the Greek letter by that name. Psi is the first letter in the Greek word *psyche,* which originally meant "soul." In modern times, it has come to be used more generally to mean "mind." Interestingly enough, the readings of Edgar Cayce identified psi with the original understanding of the word, for he insisted that "psychic" would be taken to mean "of the soul."

The concerns of parapsychology focus primarily on the development of scientific testing for the various extrasensory and psychokinetic experiences described above.

Survival Phenomena. There is a third group of paranormal occurrences that fall somewhat outside the experimental setting. These phenomena are those which relate in some way to the soul's survival of bodily death and its subsequent ability to communicate with those of us still living in this physical life. Included in this category of phenomena would be mediumship, hauntings, possession, and poltergeist activity. These paranormal occurrences are more difficult to test in a scientific setting, as they tend to occur spontaneously and cannot be induced at will quite so consistently as can ESP and PK (although the problem of spontaneity is existent to some degree in all psychic research). Attempts at scientific validation of survival phenomena have relied primarily on anecdotal evidence and consensual validation; that is, how many reliable witnesses can give the same report of an alleged paranormal event? Scientific controls attempt to rule out collusion, fraud, mass hypnosis, etc. The term psychical research has traditionally applied to this area of study, since both the British and the American Societies for Psychical Research were founded with this focus 100 years ago.

The Implications of Psi

Beyond questions concerning the controlled scientific study of psi, there lies a set of philosophical and theological questions concerning its implications. If psi is a valid human faculty or potential, what does that say about the nature of the human being? By definition, the results of parapsychological research are in conflict with known science. Psychic phenomena are *para*normal and *para*psychological because they fall outside our understood concepts of the nature of reality and the nature of the human mind.

The scientific problem with parapsychology arises from the fact that the established methods of scientific testing are based on the very understanding of the nature of reality that psi challenges. The ramifications of this problem are enormous, for if psi is genuine, then the materialistic foundation of modern science is overthrown and a new concept of reality must take its place.

The Riddle of Consciousness. Behind the testing and the gathering of statistics and the efforts to establish reliable methods of further inquiry, the essential concern of parapsychology is human consciousness. Psychology, and philosophy for centuries before it, have struggled with the knotty problem of human consciousness. What is it? How do mind and awareness relate to the body? Can consciousness exist without a brain to mediate it? Does consciousness exist in its own right, or is it merely the byproduct of the body's chemical and electrical impulses? And, if consciousness has existence in itself, how does it work through a physical being?

These questions cannot be separated from religious inquiry, for belief in the existence of a consciousness or soul is at the heart of all religious faith. It is with our consciousness that we choose God or reject Him. It is our consciousness, our awareness of ourselves, that will either survive bodily death or will not. It is on the level of consciousness that our soul ultimately has its being.

We might expect the implications of parapsychology, then, to be of burning interest to any person of religious faith. For most basically, the existence of psi would point to a realm beyond matter and physical existence. The more experimentation that is done, the more psi points to a nonmaterial world. For example, at first it was thought that perhaps some sort of electromagnetic waves were involved in telepathic communication. Such a hypothesis kept psi safely within the realm of materialistic science. Yet experimentation has indicated that physical barriers and distance do not impair telepathic function at all. Even the Soviets, who have ample motivation for explaining the phenomenon along materialistic lines, are not able to do so. Their own experiments with metal chambers and long-range telepathic communications of 600 to 5,000 kilometers have indicated that telepathy does indeed work independently of physical conditions. Research suggests that clairvoyance likewise operates in seeming independence from physical conditions, for it too is apparently unaffected by time-space considerations.

When one begins to look at precognition, the case for a nonmaterial realm becomes mind-boggling. If it is true that the mind can reach beyond the limits of time, then we are faced with some powerful implications concerning this physical world. Just what would the scientific verification of precognition suggest about time? Is it an illusion? Is the entire scope of human experience predetermined in such a way that there is a "future" already in existence which needs only to be read? Or would the "proof" of precognition suggest that our entire understanding of time is inadequate to accommodate the reality?

Psychokinesis, if genuine, carries implications no less staggering. How can a mind convert thoughts into physical action? What does this say about the capacity of spirit to act on a material world? Or the power of the human's nonphysical aspect to manifest through the physical body?

The Vital Importance of Parapsychology to Religious Issues. We do not have to reach very far to see that the philosophical considerations that make up the domain of parapsychology are at the very core of religious thought. Notwithstanding the controversy surrounding the science of parapsychology today, all indications are that it is a science growing, rather than diminishing, in respectability. We can expect the findings of parapsychology, whether ultimately valid or invalid, to have great impact on the way the world of the future views man and the universe, for the science of the day, whether right or wrong, always has been a great determinant of the prevailing worldview. (See the section on "Shifting Scientific Worldviews" in the next chapter for a discussion of this concept.) Can Christians afford to denounce or deny the field of psi? Or do they instead have a responsibility to participate—within the guidelines of their faith—in shaping the direction of this unfolding influence on our world? In the next chapter, we will examine the biblical data to see what those guidelines for participation might be.

7

The Bible's Criteria for Evaluating Psychic Experience

IN LIGHT OF the implications of parapsychology which were discussed in the last chapter, we might expect Bible-believing Christians to welcome the new science with open arms. After all, if parapsychological phenomena are genuine, then they point to the human being as a creature whose limits are far beyond those of a temporal, three-dimensional world and a physical body. They suggest that we are able to transcend the limits of ordinary time consciousness. They offer evidence that we are able to interact directly with other minds and with matter without the use of the senses or any known physical means. They promise to dethrone forever the

reigning materialistic view suggesting that we are ultimately just a bundle of chemical and electrical impulses.

In fact, it is not only concerning the nature of humans
that psychic experiences hold astounding implications,
but they go a step further and make some earthshaking
statements about the nature of reality itself. For the very
realm into which psychic experience reaches transcends
the boundaries of this world. It is a realm perhaps not
outside of time but containing time. It is a realm not necessarily excluding the material but rather including it in
a larger reality. It is a realm in which mind may work in
and through the brain, yet transcend it and live on after
the brain is dead.

In short, the implications of parapsychology support
two cornerstones of the Christian worldview: that this
world is not the only reality and that we are both a spiritual and a physical being at the same time. It offers scientific grounds for movement away from the materialism
and humanism that have so eroded Christian faith in
this century. Why, then, would any Bible-believing Christian reject parapsychology or the psychic experience
which it seeks to study? Considering all of the difficulty
that fundamental Christianity has had in defending its
supernatural claims for the Bible against the onslaught
of scientific materialism, one might expect fundamen-
talists above all others to welcome the advances of scientific *non*materialism. Yet the clergy have largely
ignored or polarized themselves against psychic experience. In fact, the most vocal opponents of things psychic
are usually to be found among the more fundamental or
Evangelical branches of Christianity.

Why Do So Many Christians Reject Psychic Experience?

There are several factors that might account for the

prevailing antipsychic climate among fundamental Christians of our day. In considering these factors, we may be inclined to think first of the warnings in the Bible concerning certain types of psychic experience. But while these warnings are an important element—and one which any biblically based position concerning psi must take into account—there are some underlying points to deal with first. Once these have been identified and considered, we will have cleared the way to examine the central question of whether the Bible does, in fact, give us a blanket prohibition against all psychic experience.

The Demonic Deception Theory. At the very foundation of Christian resistance to psi, we often find some assumptions about its origin. Discuss psychic experience with a Christian of antipsychic persuasion and you will usually find that he or she believes that all psychic experience is caused by demons, deceptive spirits, or Satan himself, presumably for the purpose of leading us away from God and into the sphere of Satanic control. If certain psychic experiences seem to bring good, that does not dissuade the staunch antipsychic Christian. And if certain psychic experiences actually bear a remarkable resemblance to a spiritual experience, that only proves the "Satanic counterfeit" explanation.

The "Satanic counterfeit" explanation of psychic experience is based on the statement in II Corinthians 11:14, that "Satan himself is transformed into an angel of light." The context is one in which the apostle Paul is warning against false teachers who masquerade as apostles of Christ. He points out that it is no wonder that such "deceitful workers" seem genuine, since even Satan can make himself appear to be an angel of light. From this warning comes the belief held among many Christians of our day that for every genuine spiritual experience Satan has a "counterfeit"—a counterfeit so convincingly like the real thing that it hoodwinks the unwary psychic dabbler into trusting in the goodness of what he or she has experienced. From there, it is easy for the devil to tighten his control, until finally he is able to take over completely. Some Christian writers have used this scenario as the explanation for how Cayce himself could have started out as a good man and eventually become so entangled that he became a messenger of the devil. (More about that in Part Three, where we will be scrutinizing Edgar Cayce as a psychic source.)

We can see how the logic of the Satanic counterfeit belief leaves no loopholes. The argument is airtight. It begins with the *a priori* supposition that psychic experience is Satanically inspired. If a psychic experience comes along that does not seem to be evil—if, for example, Edgar Cayce gives psychic information that saves someone's life—it is attributed to Satan's ability to mimic good in order to fool us. Obviously, there is no psychic experience imaginable that could break this circular argument. For if Satan himself could fool us into thinking he was an angel of light, we would be hard put to come up with an example of a psychic experience "good" enough to prove that all psychic experience is not evil! The only way we can respond to the Satanic counterfeit argument is to question its underlying assumption: *Is* all psychic experience Satanically inspired? If so, then the Satanic counterfeit theory is biblically valid. But if not, then this argument must be seen as an arbitrary and circular one.

When we study the biblical warnings concerning psychic phenomena, we will see whether they link all such manifestations to a common and Satanic origin. In the meantime, though, let's consider another factor that is sometimes behind Christian resistance to psi.

Shifting Scientific Worldviews. Another factor in

Christian resistance to psi can be traced to the church's unfortunate tendency to align itself with reigning scientific worldviews, encrusting prevailing scientific theory with theological doctrine until the two become inseparable. Probably the most notable example of this tendency is the medieval church's dogged insistence that the earth was the center of the universe (geocentricity). What began as the scientific wisdom of the day gradually became a matter of religious dogma. When the first scientific upstarts began to suggest that the earth revolved around the sun (heliocentricity), it was not only an affront to the scientific community, but also a religious heresy. For geocentricity had been bound up with notions concerning the earth as the focus of God's creation and it was blasphemous to suggest that such an earth was not the center of the universe.

By the time science had progressed to the point where heliocentricity was an incontrovertible fact, it was no easy matter to extricate church doctrine from an outmoded scientific theory. The church, therefore, became the last bastion of the geocentric fallacy. Had the church kept science and theology separate, this embarrassing situation would never have occurred. After all, what does the Bible say about geocentricity? Nothing whatsoever! Yet because they had taken *inference* from the things the Bible *does* say, the medieval theologians felt that they were defending the Word of God itself when they clung to geocentric notions.

The essential problem here is one of shifting scientific paradigms or models for understanding the world around us, and it is not so rare a problem that the controversy over geo- or heliocentricity was an isolated one. Thomas Kuhn, in his landmark work *The Structure of Scientific Revolutions* (1962), pointed out that science does not proceed indefinitely as a gradual accumulation of knowledge. Every so often, our accumulated knowledge pushes us to a brink where new information can only be accommodated by a fundamental change in the prevailing understanding of the world around us. This fundamental change is called a paradigm shift.

Accepting the sun as the center of the solar system represented a major paradigm shift four centuries ago. Abandoning the idea that the earth is flat and accepting the new paradigm of a round earth was another such change. In our own century, the discovery that time and matter are not absolute is effecting a cataclysmic paradigm shift. By its very nature, paradigm shift brings upheaval, for it introduces a worldview that is incommensurate with the one that has gone before; that is, the difficulty does not come because a new model is added to the old ones; the upheaval occurs because the new model *replaces* the old ones. It is important to notice that in each case mentioned above the shifts are made traumatic because people have tied their understanding of who they are into the prevailing beliefs about the nature of the world around them.

Because such shifts are traumatic for human society to undergo, there is a tendency to resist as long as possible and ignore or discredit the evidence that points to the coming shift. This evidence that tends to usher in a paradigm shift comes in the form of anomalies for which the reigning paradigm cannot adequately account. For example, the flat earth paradigm could not account for the way objects will disappear over the horizon or the fact that no one ever found the edge of the world. The movements of the planets in the sky presented an anomaly for the geocentric paradigm. Today, the findings of quantum physics present anomalies not adequately accounted for by scientific materialism. Parapsychological studies and near-death research present similar problems for the reigning paradigm.

For many people of our day, Christian and non-Christian alike, it is easier to ignore or discredit psychic experience than to contemplate the paradigm shift that it implies. But the real theological danger comes when well-meaning Christians link an antiparapsychological stance with biblical Christianity. It could be that once again some factions of the church have become theologically locked into the prevailing paradigm and will be among the last to make the shift that science seems to be in the throes of even now. Just as the sincere believers of medieval times were convinced that they were defending God's own revelation when they fought the heliocentric paradigm, the believers of today may be defending a soon-to-be-outmoded scientific worldview. Once identified with the old paradigm (which holds psychic manifestations to be scientifically invalid), how difficult it is for some Christians to shift to a view which acknowledges psi as a natural part of our boundless universe. Similarly, those fundamental Christians who view psi in terms of evil spirits or Satanic deception find it difficult to consider it under the daylight of modern research, which takes so much of the mystery and occult connotation away from it.

In these crucial times of scientific paradigm shift, it is essential that Christians make certain that what they are defending is truly the Bible's teaching regarding psychic experience and not just the *inference* they have made from the Bible's teaching. Once we have invested any scientific theory with theological significance, we run the risk of losing our faith if that theory is later discredited. This warning holds for both the pro-psi and anti-psi factions among Christians. Just as the anti-psi Christian runs the risk of discrediting his or her faith if psi should one day be incontrovertible scientific fact, the Christian who bases his or her faith on the evidence of psychic experience runs the risk of losing faith if cherished notions about human psychic ability are one day disproven. For this reason, it is understandable if some Christians become nervous about attempts to link psi with matters of faith. There can be a world of difference between parapsychology and spiritual experience, and we may see some Christian resistance to psi springing from this factor.

The Pitfalls of Equating the Psychic with the Spiritual. It would seem that the Bible's supernatural quality is based largely on the mystical and psychical happenings it reports. Take away the prophecies, healings, visions, and miracles and we would have a very human book. Indeed, take away the supernatural aspects of the Bible and there is very little of the Bible left intact. One Episcopal clergyman, author, and lecturer, Morton Kelsey, who is a well-known advocate of psi, has graphically demonstrated this point. Using a razor blade, he carefully removed all reports of psychic experiences from the pages of a Bible. The result is nothing short of astonishing, for the pages of his special Bible are so full of holes they look like slices of Swiss cheese!

For many advocates of psi, the numerous scriptural reports of dreams, visions, and various other extrasensory events are enough to prove the compatibility of psychic experience with the Bible. However, before we too quickly ask the Bible-based Christian to accept psychic experience as part and parcel of religious faith, there are some important distinctions and considerations to which we must be sensitive. Sometimes, in our enthusiasm for the psychic dimensions of life, we can make certain assumptions that may not be valid from the fundamental Christian's point of view.

For example, the suggestion that prayer is an experience in telepathy does not win over the antipsychic Christian. For although prayer is, in the strictest sense of the word, extrasensory communication, it is extrasensory communication with God and as such does not fit the standard definition of telepathy. Telepathy involves mind-to-mind communication, and although prayer communicates the thoughts of man to the mind of God, we would expect *God* to be telepathic! Likewise, we must be careful about assigning parapsychological significance to the life of Jesus. It may well be that He was operating according to psychic laws when He performed His miracles, but to the Christian, Jesus is in a unique position. A Christian raised in the traditions of the church would not necessarily consider Jesus' extrasensory and supernatural abilities as evidence that psi is a natural part of *our* makeup. Therefore, we can hardly use Jesus' miracles as support for modern-day psychic occurrences. Nor can we claim that parapsychology, in its general support of a nonmaterialistic paradigm, supports Christianity specifically. Contemporary psychic experience merely supports belief in spiritual life, regardless of the particular religion.

The underlying problem with most attempts to identify the supernatural aspects of the Bible with contemporary psi is that they can be reductionistic; that is, they oversimplify by attempting to take a complex event or reality and explain it in terms of a single, basic principle. The result is that something very important can be lost in the translation. For example, there is a potential danger in being too quick to explain biblical miracles in terms of psychic laws. If this practice is carried to extremes, then we will simply have a new method of explaining away all that is divine and mysterious within Scripture. In one sense, the supernatural would become the natural—and the Bible's message concerning God's transcendent power would be lost. For if we fall into thinking that biblical miracles and the experience of faith can be explained in terms of some set of psychic laws, then our view of Christian faith is in danger of becoming mechanistic.

Could parapsychology lead us to a lifeless version of Christianity that builds its faith on empirical testing rather than the movement of a living spirit? Does psychic experience lead us toward an understanding that says, "Prayer is a telepathic experience; therefore, we will research telepathy in order to increase the efficacy of our prayers"? It is partly against this tendency that some Christians have justifiably guarded themselves when they reject psi as a valid part of Christian faith.

The realization that faith is not built on scientific evidence was driven home to me some years ago, when I thought I'd found evidence for the resurrection so convincing that it could not help but lead people to faith in the risen Christ. I'd seen a remarkable presentation on the Shroud of Turin, which had not at that time generated all of the worldwide publicity it has received in the years since then. The speaker who conducted this presentation covered some points that are even today often overlooked in the numerous reports made concerning the authenticity of the Shroud. Not only did he point out many validations of the Shroud's authenticity as a first-century gravecloth of a crucified man, but he also made several salient points concerning this cloth's substantiation of the biblical story of the resurrection. For me, that was exciting evidence indeed. A cloth that supported the resurrection so convincingly could be the means of bringing people to faith in Christ, I reasoned. In my mind, there was no alternative but an affirmation of faith, once one had seen the Shroud's evidence for the resurrection.

Since this presentation concerning the Shroud was available as a slide-tape package, I suggested to my Search for God study group that we purchase this audiovisual aid in order to make similar presentations to the public. In all the years since then, and considering all the spiritually oriented presentations I have been involved with since that time, I don't think I ever approached a program with a greater sense of mission than I did that first evening our study group was to give its program on the Shroud of Turin.

Yet the effort was an abysmal failure. There was a large and riotous party going on elsewhere in the building where we met, and it drowned out what little sound our feeble tape recorder could give. In the absence of any cohesive commentary to tie the slides together, the state of our sizable audience could best be described as one of polite distraction. Needless to say, no one was any more spiritually enlightened as a result of having been there that night, and I was humiliated beyond what I could bear at the time.

At home, later, reflecting on this nightmarish evening, I tried to understand why this attempt had failed so miserably. I still felt convinced of the Shroud's authenticity and its contribution to Christian faith. I examined my motives in arranging the presentation and could honestly say that they had been good. Why, then, had it not succeeded? I prayed that I would be shown the lesson for me to learn in this experience. Then I opened my Bible at random, fully expecting an answer to this question.

The answer staring me in the face was one that was to change my entire approach to sharing my faith.

In front of me was the story of the rich man and Lazarus (Luke 16:19-31). It tells of a rich man who lived in the lap of luxury, and of Lazarus, the beggar who lay at the rich man's gates, starving and covered with sores. Both men die, the story tells us, but the rich man goes to the torment of hell, while Lazarus is carried by the angels to the bosom of Abraham. After learning that relief is impossible for himself, the rich man begs Abraham to send Lazarus to warn his brothers of what lies ahead for them unless they mend their ways. The answer the rich man is given speaks volumes on the human spirit and our oft-misguided attempts to sway it with "proof": *"If they hear not Moses and the prophets, neither will they be persuaded, though one rose from the dead."* (verse 31) I knew at once that my attempts to bring others into the fold by "proving" the resurrection had been inappropriate.

Just so, this experience taught me that it is inappropriate to use parapsychology as "proof" for Christian faith. While some psychic experiences may be seen as supportive of Christian faith (as I will attempt to show in the next section), they lose their helpfulness and become even a detriment when we allow them to substitute for our direct relationship with God.

Evaluating Modern-Day Psychic Experience

There is little point in cataloging every supernatural occurrence in the Bible. Even the most casual reader of Scripture knows that holy men of God had visions, made prophecies, and performed miracles. We can see something of the clairvoyant in a vision, recognize the precognitive nature of prophecy, and even infer the workings of psychokinetic ability in a miracle. Yet for reasons discussed in the last segment, some readers may be reluctant to link these supernatural events of the Bible with their modern-day psi equivalents. Some may even say that those Bible events were qualitatively different from the psychic experience under observation today. But are there grounds for this distinction between modern and biblical psi in the scriptural record? Bible students must admit that, according to the Bible itself, supernatural abilities were never solely the heritage of God's prophets. Even those outside the sphere of the one God's influence were at times able to produce some of the same supernatural manifestations as God's own prophets.

Pharaoh's magicians, for example, were able to duplicate Moses' miracles.

We cannot say, then, that the supernatural occurrences in the Bible were different from today's psi because they were the province of God's prophets. For, despite attempts to keep the supernatural neatly confined to the Bible, where it all took place thousands of years ago, we can see that even in biblical days all kinds of people were having various kinds of psychic experiences for a mixed assortment of motives. The evidence suggests that the very same phenomena described in Scripture are occurring today. And if in Bible times both godly and ungodly people were able to perform such feats, might we not expect the same to be true today? Perhaps the question, then, is not whether psi is biblical or not, but whether the Bible provides us criteria for evaluating modern-day psychic experience.

Heeding the Warnings. We do not have to look far to see clear and stern warnings within Scripture concerning certain occult practices:

> When thou art come into the land which the Lord thy God giveth thee, thou shalt not learn to do after the abominations of those nations. There shall not be found among you any one that maketh his son or his daughter to pass through the fire, or that useth divination, or an observer of times, or an enchanter, or a witch, or a charmer, or a consulter with familiar spirits, or a wizard, or a necromancer. For all that do these things are an abomination unto the Lord ... Deuteronomy 18:9-12

Certainly no one can deny the uncompromising prohibition that these warnings make. To anyone who has chosen the Bible as an absolute authority in matters of behavior, it is clear that certain occult practices such as divination, witchcraft, and summoning up of the dead are forbidden. The prophet Isaiah adds a further dimension to the warnings when he says: "Let now the astrologers, the stargazers, the monthly prognosticators, stand up, and save thee from these things that shall come upon thee. Behold, they shall be as stubble . . . " (Isaiah 47:13-14)

These two passages alone would seem enough to justify the position that psychically oriented practices are not only worthless but are also an "abomination" to God. That's pretty strong wording and should not be taken lightly. Understandably, it is on these warnings that the antipsychic position is most often based. But, clear as these prohibitions are, do they apply to *all* psychic experiences? Is everyone who is involved in things psychic committing an abomination? Are those who accept and work with certain types of psychic information in the wrong, biblically speaking, while those who denounce it are in the right? Must we take a black-or-white, good-or-evil view of psychic phenomena, or is there a middle ground? I believe there is ample biblical data to suggest that there *is* an alternative. And it is an alternative often overlooked by those who make a blanket condemnation of psychic experience, as well as by those who indiscriminately hail all psychic experience as God-sent. The alternative? We might simply regard psychic phenomena as a manifestation of that which is nonmaterial in humans and consider them neither good nor evil in themselves.

Psychic Ability as a Neutral Soul Faculty. Christians universally accept the existence of a soul. Isn't it reasonable to link psi, the capacity to know and communicate through means other than the five senses, to this nonphysical component of the human being? The fact that the Bible and even personal observation may present cases where psychic ability is used destructively does not in itself prove that psychic power is a bad thing. There are many areas of life where misuse makes a neutral or even potentially good force destructive. God gave us dominion over the earth, for example, but consider what we have done with *that* power. The creative and the destructive alike spring from man as he exercises the God-given prerogative of dominion over the earth. The fact that there is often misuse of psychic capabilities does not make psychic ability bad, any more than misuse of our bodies makes the flesh inherently evil.

Nonetheless, in the light of the warning passages given above, is there room for a neutral view of psi? Doesn't the scriptural record come down so firmly on the anti-psi side of the argument that we are only fooling ourselves to suggest that a Christian can accept the potential goodness of psychic experience? Not necessarily. Those warnings represent only half the picture. Further reading in that same Bible will indicate that many psychic events are reported in a positive light.

The Other Biblical Perspective on Psi. In I Samuel 9:9 there is found this interesting piece of information: " . . . he that is now called a Prophet was beforetime called a Seer." The equation between clairvoyance (being a "seer") and the general Old Testament definition of the word "prophet" is striking. Still, there may be a tendency to separate biblical accounts of prophets "being in the spirit" or of those which state, "I was in a vision" (for example, the openings of the books of Amos, Hosea, Joel, Micah, Nahum, John's revelation, and even the account of Peter's trance at Joppa as reported in Acts 10) from the mundane modern versions of clairvoyance and precognition. But before we make too much of this apparent distinction between the biblical label of "prophet" and the contemporary term "psychic," we should take another look at that passage in I Samuel 9 which defines a seer. It relates the story of how Saul (later to become the first king of Israel) met up with Samuel, one of the greatest of Israel's prophets. The account tells us that Saul went to Samuel the prophet in order to get help in finding some lost asses! Thus we find the great prophet Samuel functioning as a clairvoyant. Apparently God did not object to this use of Samuel's psychic perception, for it was in the context of this historic meeting that the first king of Israel was anointed by God's prophet!

Prophets and Psychics. If it seems wrong somehow to equate the words "prophet" and "psychic," we should remember that the Bible talks about just as many false prophets as it does true ones. Prophet, then, is in itself a neutral label that can be applied to one who uses his special extrasensory ability to work in accordance with God's will or to one who uses this ability to counter God's will. Thus, the "true" or "false" labels used in connection with prophets apply not so much to whether one indeed has extrasensory abilities as to how those abilities are used. For those Christians of today who are trying to sort out the arguments for and against psychic experience, this scriptural distinction between the true and the false prophet can be a key. It is actually from this basic distinction that we can begin to extract principles from the biblical data that will tell us how to evaluate similar manifestations in this day and age.

Let's return, then, to those scriptural warnings concerning psychic manifestations to see what else they may have to tell us about the proper and improper use of psi:

And when they shall say unto you, Seek unto

them that have familiar spirits, and unto wizards that peep, and that mutter: *should not a people seek unto their God?* (author's italics) Isaiah 8:19

A Standard for Evaluating Psychic Experience. Contained within this verse is the essence of the entire biblical message concerning psychic manifestation: It does not just forbid engagement in certain psychic practices, but it tells us why. When we turn to occult sources for the nurture, guidance, and direction that we should seek from our God, we are turning away from God. The destructive nature of such a substitution is obvious. Similarly, in the passage from Isaiah 47 given earlier, we cannot avoid the implication that the people had come to look to their astrologers and prognosticators for that which they should have been seeking from their God. An earlier verse in the Isaiah 47 passage says:

Thy wisdom and thy knowledge, it hath perverted thee; and thou hast said in thine heart, I am, and none else beside me. Verse 10

What a clear picture of a people who have come to rely on their own abilities, knowledge, and wisdom instead of a direct relationship with God! But does a misguided dependence on something make it bad in itself? Does the verse above suggest that wisdom and knowledge are bad, or that the people's apparently arrogant *faith* in their wisdom and knowledge was the problem? This seems a far more reasonable explanation of Isaiah 47:10, and of verses 13 and 14 as well. For when considering the denunciation of astrologers contained in the latter passage, it is only fair to look at the New Testament account that tells us that the Wise Men (translated "astrologers" in the New English and New American versions) were guided to the Christ child because they understood

the sign of the star in the heavens. In one case, a misuse
of astrological knowledge led the people away from their
God and to destruction. In the other, it led them to the
feet of the Messiah.

The lesson here is an important one. It demonstrates
to us that the way we use certain types of knowledge is
the significant factor in evaluating its acceptability before God. The passages in Isaiah strongly suggest that
this applies to any kind of knowledge, be it spiritual,
secular, esoteric, or psychic. Even the warnings in
Deuteronomy carry this same message. After forbidding
the children of Israel to participate in certain psychic
activities, the Lord goes on to explain *why:*

> For these nations, which thou shalt possess,
> hearkened unto observers of times, and unto divin-
> ers: but as for thee, the Lord thy God hath not suf-
> fered thee to do so. The Lord thy God will raise up
> unto thee a Prophet from the midst of thee, of thy
> brethren, like unto me; unto him ye shall
> hearken . . . Deuteronomy 18:14-15

Once again we see psychic practices forbidden because there is a better way. The reference to God raising
up a prophet may be seen as a prophecy concerning the
coming Messiah, thus identifying the Christ with the alternative to dependence on psychic practices. It is interesting to note the phrase, "from the midst of thee, of thy
brethren." For although this in the literal refers to the
Messianic line, it also reminds us of the nearness of the
presence of God. On this point the Cayce readings are
explicit, advising us:

> For as the pattern was given even in the mount of
> old, when ye turn to Him, He will direct thee. Why,
> O Why, then, [turn] to any subordinate, when thy

brother, thy Christ, thy Savior would speak with thee! 1299-1

The seeking of God and reliance on Christ were given time and time again in the readings of Edgar Cayce as the alternative to psychic dabbling. Not that psychic information or even the development of psychic ability within oneself was discredited, but that all psychic experience should be measured against an exacting standard, the same standard given in the Bible: Does the information or the experience lead you toward God or away from Him? For example, this advice was given to one person seeking direction in the development of her psychic abilities:

> As we find, in defining then for the entity those questions, there must first be the purport—there must be the answer only within self—as to whom ye will serve. Is it God or man? Is it self or fame or fortune? Are there those grounds for common meeting of these influences?
>
> For as the Teacher of teachers gave, as all who have pointed to a service to their fellow men, there is *one* God; or "The Lord thy God is *one*"—and the expression should be, "My Spirit (not spirits, but *my* Spirit) beareth witness with *thy* spirit (not spirits) as to whether ye be the child of God or not." 1376-1

The implication is clear that only psychic awareness that puts us in touch with the Spirit of the one God is appropriate. The readings of Edgar Cayce and the Bible seem to agree on this point, for we have the same central criterion as expressed in Deuteronomy:

> If there arise among you a prophet, or a dreamer of dreams, and giveth thee a sign or a wonder, And

the sign or the wonder come to pass, whereof he spake unto thee, saying, Let us go after other gods, which thou hast not known, and let us serve them; Thou shalt not hearken unto the words of that prophet, or that dreamer of dreams: for the Lord your God proveth you, to know whether ye love the Lord your God with all your heart and with all your soul. Ye shall walk after the Lord your God, and fear him, and keep his commandments, and obey his voice, and ye shall serve him, and cleave unto him. And that prophet, or that dreamer of dreams, shall be put to death; because he hath spoken to turn you away from the Lord your God, which brought you out of the land of Egypt, and redeemed you out of the house of bondage . . . Deuteronomy 13:1-5

The language is strong here, disconcertingly strong for many of us today; but the message comes through loud and clear: We may evaluate psychic information on the basis of its effect on our relationship with God. Does it draw us closer to Him or does it lure us away? That which lures us away is indeed so destructive as to merit the appellation, abomination.

This point is very important, for it tells us that it is not the psychic manifestation itself which we are to condemn. Instead, we are to look at its effect—*and* the motivation of the prophet or psychic. This principle is consistent with the entire biblical record of psychic events, for this record often juxtaposes good and bad examples of the same psychic manifestation. What was the difference between Moses' feats before Pharaoh and those of the Egyptian magicians? The objective phenomena were the same. Yet Moses was acting as a tool of God and the Egyptians were practicing magic. In II Kings 17:3 God testifies against Israel by all the prophets, using them as His spokesmen. But Jeremiah 23:16 says, "Hearken not unto the words of the prophets that prophesy unto you: they make you vain: they speak a vision of their own heart, and not out of the mouth of the Lord."

What sets these prophets apart from those speaking for God? Verse 14 tells us that " . . . they commit adultery, and walk in lies: they strengthen also the hands of evil-doers . . . " In other words, their spiritual integrity leaves much to be desired. Still, the Lord does not on this basis condemn *all* prophets, but rather asks, "What is the chaff to the wheat?" (verse 28) Likewise, in the New Testament (Acts 13:6-11) we find Paul encountering the sorcerer Barjesus, and he calls him the "child of the devil." (verse 10) But in the same book we are told of Agabus, the good prophet who accurately predicts a famine. (Acts 11:28)

Psychic Practices Forbidden in the Bible. In each of the examples above, we can see a positive and a negative use of the same psychic ability. This is not to say, however, that *all* psychic practices are allowed by Scripture provided we use them correctly. There are certain practices that we never see presented in a positive light within the Bible. Communication with the dead and witchcraft are among them. The Cayce readings clearly concur with the scriptural message concerning these practices. All forms of communication with the dead are discouraged in the readings, and concerning "interests in the mystic, the psychic, the occult forces" Cayce warns:

> *Do not confuse them!* For that as becomes applicable in thine experience must be prompted by the desire, the wish within self, and that in accordance with divine ideals.

> What, then, *is* thine ideal? Is it founded in that ye yourself may do, or that in which ye may be the *channel* through which others may find *their* association with a *living* God . . . 1265-1

While some writers have mistakenly called Edgar Cayce a spiritist medium, he in fact did not channel the messages of discarnate beings in order to get his information. (More about this in Part Three.) Far from being mediumistic in nature, Edgar Cayce's readings actually warn that attempts to communicate with the dead may lead us to encounter dangerous or deceptive spiritual beings or forces. As one person was advised, "Seek not other entities . . . not that there is not the communion of saints, but there is also the communion of sinners! Ye seek not those!" The advice also contained a reminder about the importance of keeping all psychic development centered around an ideal: "In thy application, then—first know thy ideal. As has been indicated, ye have chosen well; but know Him as thy friend, as thy brother, as thy Savior." (2787-1)

There was another reason the Cayce readings gave for avoiding seances and similar attempts to get information from discarnate entities. These readings point out that there is no reason to assume that the souls of the dead are any wiser than they were while on earth. In passing on to the after-death state, we hold on to our biases and misinformation right along with our beliefs and our positive traits. As Cayce so colorfully put it:

> For do not consider for a moment . . . that an individual soul-entity passing from an earth plane as a Catholic, a Methodist, an Episcopalian, is something else because he is dead! He's only a dead Episcopalian, Catholic or Methodist. 254-92

Furthermore, our attempts to communicate with the dead can be disruptive to the well-being of the souls we seek to call up from the after-death state. In the Bible story of Saul and the witch of Endor (I Samuel 28), we find that when Saul goes to the woman with familiar spirits (spirit guides) and asks her to conjure up the spirit of the departed Samuel, Samuel is none too pleased to be brought forth: "And Samuel said to Saul, Why hast thou disquieted me, to bring me up?" (verse 15)

Saul was fortunate that he had nothing worse than Samuel's disapproval to deal with, for we are extremely vulnerable to deception and perhaps spiritual and psychological harm when we open up to communicate with the dead. Psychic perception is a two-way street, and if we have any thought of receiving information from spirits, we must open ourselves up to them. Opening up to the spirit world can be a dangerous thing to do. Just as there are people with good and bad intentions in physical life, there are also "people" (spirits) with good and bad intentions on the "other side." Hence the justifiable warning that we keep our guard against deceptive or evil spirits. There is no guarantee that the voice that identifies itself as a departed loved one is truly that person.

Cautions on the Use of All Psychic Information. Aside from the pitfalls that make spirit communication a psychic practice to avoid, there are other cautions that should be a part of the biblically based approach to psi. The careful weighing of all psychic information against the standard of one's faith is essential for any Christian who chooses to accept the dimension of psi as a part of spiritual life. How many times have we given or received advice that was misleading—despite the sincerity and the good intentions behind the advice? Just so, we must recognize that psychic information is rarely 100 percent accurate. It passes through our minds or the minds of the psychic delivering the information and may become distorted along the way. If we assume that a piece of information or a doctrine is valid simply because it came in a psychic fashion, we are bound for disappointment and trouble. And we have fallen into the trap that Scripture warns against.

Isn't It Easier and Safer to Just Stay Away from Psi?
This thought certainly has appeal. Yet if we avoid or denounce all psychic experience, aren't we denying the very foundation of the *good* supernatural within the Bible? If God once spoke to people through dreams and visions, is there any reason to suppose that He no longer does? If seers could once "shew us our way that we should go" (I Samuel 9:6), why would we expect that God has abolished that function? After all, doesn't that great prophecy in the book of Joel promise us that "your sons and your daughters shall prophesy, your old men shall dream dreams, your young men shall see visions . . . "? (Joel 2:28) Lest we think that this statement is reserved for major prophetic events and is not intended to apply to the day-by-day help that can come from psychic experience, we should consider this wisdom from Job:

> For God speaketh once, yea twice, yet man perceiveth it not. In a dream, in a vision of the night, when deep sleep falleth upon men, in slumberings upon the bed; Then he openeth the ears of men, and sealeth their instruction . . . Job 33:14-16

Doesn't this passage suggest that God is ready to guide and direct us through the channels of our own subconscious minds? When a television evangelist tells us that a woman in Wisconsin is being healed of crippling arthritis at that very moment, is he not allowing God-given psychic information to come through his own subconscious mind? Yes, this incident may be different from clairvoyance used for selfish purposes, but such disparity in the uses of psi can be traced back to Bible times. In dealing with psychic perception, we must be ready to recognize what is of God and what is not.

Always we return to the central importance of evaluating all psychic experience and information. Like so many things in life, psi presents us with the opportunity to choose, to sharpen our powers of discernment, and to make constructive use of the best abilities that God has put at our disposal. A summary set of criteria for doing this will be presented in the next chapter.

8

A Tenable Position for
the Biblically Centered Christian

IN THE LAST two chapters, we have explored the various types of modern-day psychic experience, considered their implications, and evaluated psi against the biblical record. If the work of Edgar Cayce is to have any place in the life of the Christian who accepts the Bible as the final word of doctrinal authority, it must first be because that Christian has found a tenable position concerning psi in general. Once proper criteria for working with psi under biblical direction have been established, the work of Edgar Cayce as a particular psychic can be evaluated against those criteria.

A Summary of the Biblical Data Concerning Psi

In developing a Christian perspective on psi, we might summarize the biblical data as follows:

1. The Bible contains numerous accounts of psychic happenings. In fact, remove the psychic dimension from the Bible, and you will find a very human book.

2. The Bible contains clear and imposing warnings concerning certain psychic practices, notably those that involve witchcraft and communication with spirits of the dead.

3. The Bible also reports many instances where psychic functioning occurs with God's blessing.

4. Evaluating the biblical data that deals with true and false prophets, as well as examples where the same psychic manifestation was used for good and for evil, we may conclude that psychic ability is a neutral force that may be used constructively or destructively.

5. Psychic information or experience is destructive when it leads us away from our faith.

6. Psychic information or ability is destructive when we come to depend on it.

7. Psychic information or ability is destructive when we allow it to take the place of God in our lives.

8. Psi, used properly, is at the very foundation of our spiritual nature. It can be an avenue of acknowledging and expressing the spirit in a material world.

9. Psi, used properly, can be a means of communication with, receiving instruction from, and being used by God.

10. It is our responsibility to evaluate psychic information and experience in order to determine whether it is (a) consistent with our faith, (b) leads us toward rather than away from God, and (c) has a constructive influence on our lives.

11. The spiritual integrity of a psychic source plus the information that source presents are factors to weigh when evaluating psychic information.

A Standard for Evaluating

Whenever we evaluate something, it must be against a standard of some sort. This is probably one of the reasons that we are urged by the Cayce readings to set an ideal for our lives. That ideal, then, becomes a reliable standard of measurement by which we can evaluate not only our own progress in spiritual life, but also whatever advice or "guidance" comes our way—be it from a psychic, spiritual, or secular source. The Bible, too, emphasizes the importance of a standard. In I John 4:1 we are told, " . . . believe not every spirit, but try the spirits whether they are of God . . . " Then John goes on to give us a standard of measurement: "Every spirit that confesseth that Jesus Christ is come in the flesh is of God . . . " (verse 2)

In this standard given by John, we see the continuation of the same standard suggested in the Old Testament book of Deuteronomy: Will we choose that which points to the Prophet, the Messiah, the Christ, our *direct* contact with God, or will we sacrifice that supreme opportunity in favor of practices which lead us away from

Him? For the biblically centered Christian, this is the central, the only, criterion upon which to evaluate any experience or information. If a given psychic manifestation measures up favorably against *this* measuring rod, who can say that it is wrong?

Part
Three

Edgar Cayce as a Psychic Source

9

Examining the Source

TO SUMMARIZE THE postulation of the last two chapters, psychic experience and information are biblically acceptable if they are worked with under certain guidelines. As we go on to examine Edgar Cayce as a specific source of psychic information, then we may apply those criteria developed in chapters 7 and 8 to determine the acceptability of the Cayce information when it is measured against biblical standards. Using those guidelines, we can approach our examination of the Edgar Cayce readings with the following steps:

As a starting point, we can apply Jeremiah's criterion concerning the source's spiritual integrity, looking at what we know of the life of Edgar Cayce to see if he measures up favorably against the standards of conduct that Jeremiah sets for an acceptable psychic source. This most basic criterion being met, we can then go on to examine the nature of Edgar Cayce's *psychic* functioning to see if it falls among those activities prohibited in Scripture, or if it is among those which are acceptable within the biblical guidelines. Assuming that these two initial criteria are met, we will then go on to the last, crucial test: How does the psychic information that Edgar Cayce gave compare with the teachings of the Bible?

The first two criteria will make up the content of this chapter. The last one will be covered in some depth throughout the remainder of this book. First, then, let's take a look at Edgar Cayce's spiritual integrity.

What Do We Know About Edgar Cayce, the Man?

It would be redundant to include even an abbreviated version of the Edgar Cayce story in this work. Presumably, anyone who had enough interest in the subject of this book to pick it up and read this far would already have known something of the Cayce story. For those who require more information concerning the biographical details of Edgar Cayce's life, that story is a matter of public record and can be found in a number of sources. (For a listing of book titles, check the books and tapes catalog from the A.R.E. Press as well as main titles in the A.R.E. Library.) For our purposes, I will focus on several events and circumstances in Edgar Cayce's life that will shed light on our understanding of him as a psychic source. First, it would seem that a consideration of the main issues and events related to Edgar Cayce's discovery and use of his gift are germane to the question of this psychic's spiritual integrity.

Edgar Cayce's Discovery of His Gift. We know that from early childhood Edgar Cayce was a religious boy, whose spiritual nature expressed itself in a keen interest in the Bible. At the tender age of ten, he decided to read the Bible from cover to cover one time for every year of his life. That was a rather unusual decision for a young boy to make. More unusual still, he followed through on his decision. He read long portions daily until he had caught up to his age, for he had ten years to make up. Finally, at the age of twelve, Edgar Cayce had read the Bible through twelve times.

This practice was not something Cayce adopted in order to set a record, nor was it an empty gesture for him, but an honest attempt to grow in understanding of God's word. As a child, the young Edgar had listened to adults arguing theological issues, using their relative familiarity with the Bible to back their positions. Edgar decided then and there that, if he read the Bible from cover to cover every year of his life, that would be the best guidance possible concerning spiritual truth.

It was when Edgar had completed that twelfth reading of his Bible that his now-famous vision occurred. A woman appeared to him, told him that his prayers had been answered, and asked him what he would like. Now it seems to me that those who claim that Edgar Cayce's childhood psychic experiences were the beginnings of a Satanic deception are faced with a difficult question. It is a question similar to the one I raised in telling my own story: How could this child who earnestly sought God's guidance, looked to the Bible for truth, and trusted in God to lead him, be led by the devil instead? If it is possible for the devil to swoop in under those circumstances and take us into his clutches—right out from under God's nose—how terribly vulnerable we all are! What chance do we really have to find truth, if demonic deception can enter as a response to our prayers to God?

Why, we might also ask, did Edgar Cayce respond to his vision the way he did, if this experience was an ungodly one? He asked for nothing selfish. He asked for no psychic gifts, no unusual powers. Instead, he said he wanted to grow up to help sick people, especially children. From that time on, his boyhood aspiration was to be a medical missionary. Hardly the outcome we'd expect from a Satanically inspired vision.

Indications of the Man's Spiritual Integrity. As Edgar Cayce grew into adulthood, all reports indicate that he continued to be a person of high spiritual integrity. As his psychic gift emerged and developed, he sought guidance in his Bible and in his prayer life. Much is made in some of the Christian anti-Cayce materials of the soul-searching and spiritual struggle that Cayce periodically went through during the course of his life. But does the fact that he sometimes questioned his abilities and their source make him less a person of spiritual integrity, or does it make him more of one? Is unwavering confidence in the rightness of one's own beliefs and actions proof of one's faith or proof of one's unwillingness to be shown wrong? To those who see Edgar Cayce's wrestling with his gift and his questioning of some of the new concepts that emerged through it as proof that he knew deep down inside that he was going astray, I submit that his soul-searching was instead evidence that he never stopped being willing to let God show him if he were wrong.

As we examine further Edgar Cayce's spiritual integrity, we see a man who repeatedly resisted the temptations that his psychic ability presented to him. Wealth and power were continually available to him through his psychic gift, for example, yet he availed himself of neither.

This is not to say that Cayce or those who knew him best have tried to create the image of a modern-day saint. By all reports, he was an ordinary man with normal shortcomings. But then again, so have all of God's servants from the beginning of time been normal people with normal failings. When we scrutinize the question of Edgar Cayce's integrity as a psychic source, the important point is not to look for a saint, but to ask whether he was someone who tried to live within the dictates of Christian ethics and morality, as well as the leadings of his own conscience. While no one connected with the work of Edgar Cayce should attempt to place him on a spiritual pedestal, we can assert without reservation that we are looking at a man who led a simple, moral, and God-centered life. A far cry from Jeremiah's description of false prophets who "commit adultery, and walk in lies: [and] strengthen also the hands of evildoers . . . " (Jeremiah 23:14)

Throughout his life, Edgar Cayce the man remained active in his church, was an inspiring Sunday school teacher, and commanded the liking and respect of those who knew him. It is interesting to note that even his most vociferous Christian critics will usually concede that he was a good man with good intentions. If there were any shameful chapters in the life of this great psychic, we can be sure they would have been uncovered and well publicized by his critics by now. Instead, the supposed error in Edgar Cayce's ways is nearly always attributed not to evil but to his being misguided.

Edgar Cayce's Walk with Jesus. Finally, before we move from consideration of Edgar Cayce the man to consideration of his psychic gift itself, let's take just a glimpse at the man's personal relationship with Jesus. Cayce called himself a Christian. Those who knew him considered him a Christian. Some Christian writers have questioned whether this was indeed true. Some writers have suggested that he started out as a faithful Christian, but then slipped away somewhere along the line. In response to those charges, I include here an excerpt from Edgar Cayce's personal correspondence. This letter was written in 1932, late in Cayce's psychic career, and well after the time when he would have allegedly lost his Christian faith. Someone had apparently written to him, sharing a personal experience with Christ, for Mr. Cayce responded:

... often I have felt, seen and heard the Master at hand. Just a few days ago I had an experience which I have not even told the folk here. As you say, they are too scary to tell, and we wonder at ourselves when we attempt to put them into words, whether we are to believe our own ears, or if others feel we are exaggerating or drawing on our imagination; but to us indeed they are often that which we feel if we hadn't experienced we could not have gone on.

The past week I have been quite "out of the running," but Wednesday afternoon when going into my little office or den for the 4:45 meditation, as I knelt by my couch I had the following experience: First a light gradually filled the room with a golden glow, that seemed to be very exhilarating, putting me in a buoyant state. I felt as if I were being given a healing. Then, as I was about to give the credit to members of our own group who meet at this hour for meditation (as I felt each and every one of them were praying for and with me), *He* came. He stood before me for a few minutes in all the glory that He must have appeared in to the three on the Mount. Like yourself, I heard the voice of my Jesus say, "Come unto me and rest." Supplement to 281-13

The Source of Edgar Cayce's Psychic Information

When we examine the life of the man Edgar Cayce, the evidence seems clear enough that he passes the first test of a psychic source. His spiritual integrity is generally unquestioned even by his critics. But what of the next test? When we examine the nature of Edgar Cayce's psychic functioning, do we find his psychic gift to fall among those practices forbidden by Scripture? With regard to this question, most Christian critics of Edgar Cayce charge that he was a spiritist medium. This is a very important claim to investigate. For if Cayce sought and consulted discarnate spirits in order to get his information, then he was clearly in violation of the guidelines set down in Scripture. We should examine the Cayce readings carefully, then, to see just what we can discover about the source of this great volume of psychic information.

Edgar Cayce's Psychic Functioning Was Not Mediumistic in Nature. Contrary to some allegations, Cayce did not consult "familiar spirits" when he went into his altered state to receive information. He did not call, conjure, or seek contact with the spirits of the dead. Rather, he entered an unconscious state of awareness that apparently put him in touch with other minds and something like a "universal intelligence," as we shall see shortly.

It is true that on occasion Edgar Cayce encountered the spirits of the deceased, as well as beings who identified themselves as angels, while he was in the unconscious (or sleeplike) state that enabled him to give a reading. Much emphasis has been placed on this fact in the literature that attempts to demonstrate that Cayce was a medium. But does the mere encountering of a discarnate soul or a nonphysical being make one a medium?

At first the answer to this question may seem to be, "Yes, of course, it does." After all, there are recorded instances in the Cayce readings in which a nonphysical personality conveys a message via the sleeping psychic. Does not this make him a medium? Not necessarily. There is an important distinction we must make between Cayce's occasional contact in consciousness with a nonphysical being and a mediumistic function. First, these occurrences were the exception rather than the rule. In the more than 14,000 psychic readings, only a handful indicate such contact. Secondly, and most important, Edgar Cayce *did not seek these entities as the source of his information.*

If this distinction seems to be merely a technical one, having no bearing on the issue at stake, how are we to understand the scriptural accounts of Mary, Joseph, and countless others in Scripture being spoken to by angels? Were they not receiving information from nonphysical beings who identified themselves as angels? When we read of the transfiguration of Jesus on the mountain (Matthew 17), what do we read, but that Jesus and His disciples encounter the discarnate spirits of Moses and Elijah! Interestingly enough, it was not the sight of the long-dead prophets that frightened Jesus' disciples, but the voice of God when He says, "This is my beloved Son, in whom I am well pleased; hear ye him." (verse 5) It would seem, then, that there is good biblical precedent for the spontaneous, unsought encounter with a nonphysical being, be it angel or discarnate human soul. Such encounters are no more mediumistic than is the spontaneous dream or vision of a departed loved one the same as a seance. The distinguishing characteristic is that the men and women in Scripture who encountered such nonphysical beings did so spontaneously, in the course of doing or being receptive to God's will. They were not seeking or conjuring nonphysical beings.

By the same token, we can see that, when Cayce went into his altered state, he was bound to encounter those who had passed on from time to time. He was moving his conscious awareness out of this physical world and into the nonphysical realms where some disincarnate souls might well be dwelling. Yet the overwhelming evidence, when we examine the readings, is that he did not seek spirit entities as the source of his information. His voice did not change during a reading, as that of a trance medium typically does. Those with him did not "see" the spirits of the departed materialize in the room. Also worth noting is that, in those rare cases where a specific nonphysical personality had information to convey, it identified itself. In contrast, we have the vast majority of readings where no such source is identified.

Finally, and possibly most important, we have the readings' own tendency to discourage people from seeking to make contact with spirits of the dead. Some of these admonitions and the reasons behind them we have already considered in chapter 7. While there is little point in repeating those excerpts here, we can add the following pieces of advice from the Cayce readings concerning the use of spirit "guides":

When one person asked in his reading, "What leader or teacher could guide [the] body along the path?" the response came:

> *Him!* In Him! Along the ways that were given by Him! Be satisfied with nothing less than He as thy guide, by day and by night! Let ever that mind be in thee: *"If His presence abides not with me day by day, may I not be lifted up!"* 452-6

In the same vein, another person who was looking for enlightenment from the entities of the spirit world was advised:

Seek not other than that of His meeting thee within thine own temple. For beside Him there is none other. Know, as He gave, they that climb up some other way are robbers.

Then, listen—listen to that voice within. Prepare thyself, consecrate thyself, purify [thyself] . . . He stands and knocks. Will ye entertain Him? Then, do not entertain others. 2029-1

If Edgar Cayce's readings were being provided by discarnate spirits that sought to speak through him, why, we might ask, did they discourage people from seeking contact with them? It would seem that the conclusion that Cayce's information did not come from discarnate spirits is far more in keeping with the evidence.

What Was Edgar Cayce's Source? If we rule out spirit entities as the source of Edgar Cayce's information, the next question to arise is, what *was* the source of this information? Not surprisingly, Cayce himself was asked this question many times, and the question was put to the readings on numerous occasions. From the answers given, it seems we can conclude that there were two main sources of Edgar Cayce's psychic information.

In many cases, his information came through what might be described as a telepathic functioning. Particularly in the physical readings, he apparently read the unconscious mind of the person seeking help in order to get the physical diagnosis. The underlying assumption here is that we each, on the unconscious level, are perfectly aware of what is taking place within our own bodies. Modern research into hypnosis tends to bear out this assumption. Applied to Cayce's psychic functioning, this principle suggests that, in giving his physical diagnoses, Cayce was merely telepathically receiving what the other person's unconscious mind already knew about his or her body's condition.

Taking the telepathic function a step further, we can note that Cayce's ability to tap unconscious minds apparently was not limited to the mind of the person receiving the reading. Often we find indications of an astounding ability to pick up telepathically information from the minds of third parties and apply that information to the needs of the person being diagnosed. The most well-known example of this extended telepathic ability is the story of Cayce's meeting with Dr. Harold Reilly, a New York City physiotherapist. Long before Cayce had ever heard of Dr. Reilly, his readings began recommending Reilly's physical therapies for several health reading recipients in the New York area. Unbeknownst to the conscious Cayce, it just so happened that Dr. Reilly, who had a health institute at Rockefeller Center, practiced many of the same physical therapies that the readings repeatedly recommended. It seems that Edgar Cayce was able to perceive telepathically or clairvoyantly what he needed to know about Dr. Reilly's therapies in order to "match" them with the physical needs of the person receiving the reading. Cayce's readings had been sending people to Reilly for several years before the two men finally met for the first time.

In another case, we see a similar telepathic matching, this time of a patient's need with a medicinal formula that existed in the mind of a third person. Many of the remedies Cayce recommended in his health readings were hard-to-find, nonprescription, and patent medicines. In this particular instance, the search for an unheard-of preparation recommended in a health reading proved fruitless. Consequently, an ad was placed in a medical journal, asking for information concerning the availability of this item. When response was not soon forthcoming, Cayce was asked to provide the formula for this preparation in a psychic reading, as he had already shown an ability to give such formulas as part of the psychic discourse. The formula was given accordingly. Shortly after that, a letter arrived from France, where the medical journal ad had been noted by the son of a man who had indeed formulated such a preparation. The preparation had never been manufactured, and there were no plans to do so, and the man who formulated it had since died. In his reply to the ad, the son included the formula his father had developed. It matched the one Edgar Cayce had given in his reading.

Mind-to-mind communication, gleaning pertinent facts and circumstances, and presenting them in a helpful composite—these seemed to be the nature of Edgar Cayce's psychic functioning. In fact, we see this very concept described in one reading that discusses the source of Cayce's psychic information:

"In this [altered] state the conscious mind becomes subjugated to the subconscious, superconscious or soul mind" (3744-3), the explanation begins, pointing out that when in his sleeplike state, Cayce's conscious awareness was tuned in to the part of his own mind that had higher awareness. The explanation continues:

" . . . and [this superconscious or soul mind] may and does communicate with like minds . . . " Here we see the telepathic function, the attuning of Edgar Cayce's superconscious mind with other superconscious minds. Once in a state where such communication becomes possible, "the subconscious or soul force becomes universal," we are next told.

What does this mean? It seems to suggest that when one has the potential to communicate with all other superconscious minds, one's awareness does in truth take on universal proportions.

Some Christian writers, in acknowledging the astounding accuracy of Edgar Cayce's readings, assert that such knowledge is "superhuman" and, therefore, demonic in origin. But was it really so "superhuman"? It was, if we consider only the content of one man's (Edgar Cayce's) mind. But when we imagine him tapping the cumulative knowledge of countless other minds through a well-developed telepathic ability, the "superhuman" knowledge seems far more human and far more comprehensible. The next sentence of the reading underscores this concept and adds yet another thought concerning the source of the Cayce information:

"From any subconscious mind information may be obtained, either from this plane or from the impressions as left by the individuals that have gone on before, as we see a mirror reflecting direct that which is before it." (3744-3) There is an interesting possibility suggested in this last sentence. Not only could Edgar Cayce's mind tune in to the *minds* of people who were living and thinking at the time when he gave his readings, but it could also pick up impressions left *behind* by the thoughts of those who were now gone from this world. Note that this was not at all the same as spirit communication, for he specified: "It is not the object [mind of the person who has gone before] itself, but that reflected, as in this: The suggestion that reaches through to the subconscious or soul, in this state, gathers information from that as reflected from what has been or is called real or material . . . " (3744-3)

This last statement may not be the clearest comment ever made in the Cayce material, but if we examine it closely I think we can find a valuable clue concerning the source of much of Edgar Cayce's information. How might we understand this process of gathering "information from that as reflected from what has been . . . real or material"? An analogy from physical science may help here.

Every elementary school science class teaches that the light waves from which we pick up visual images travel forever out into the universe. Some of the stars we see in the sky at night may be long dead, for example. They only appear to be there now because the light waves of those stars are just now finding their way across billions of miles to the earth. A graphic example of this point is often made in the statement that, if we could go far enough out into the universe and had the proper telescopic equipment, we could see George Washington crossing the Delaware. The idea that events leave their impressions behind, whether in light waves or in the more esoteric "reflections" Edgar Cayce spoke about, suggests that there is an unseen record of everything that has ever happened. That record is there to be "read" by anyone who is in the proper position to do so. When Edgar Cayce perceived some of his psychic information, he was apparently doing the psychic equivalent of going far enough out into the universe to see Washington crossing the Delaware.

We can get further clarification from other readings, which discuss this unseen record in greater detail:

> From what source, or how, is such a record read of the activities in the past? How may self know that there is being given a *true* record of the activities in a period of which there is no written *word* [of] history? Yet the entity itself . . . is studying, the records that are written in nature, in the rocks, in the hills, in the trees, in that termed the genealogical log of nature itself. Just as true, then, is the record that the mind makes upon the film of time and space in the activities of a body . . . 487-17

This record on the "film" of time and space is elsewhere in the Cayce readings and in other traditions called the "Akashic record," taken from the Hindu word *akasha,* meaning "sky"; thus, the somewhat poetic image of a record being written on the sky. The readings tie this concept in to a rather traditional Judeo-Christian image, too, when they give this description:

> Upon time and space is written the thoughts, the deeds, the activities of an entity . . . Hence, as it has been oft called, the record is God's book of remembrance . . . 1650-1

We find a strikingly similar concept in several passages from both the Old and New Testaments. In the Fifty-Sixth Psalm, for example, the psalmist addresses God's knowledge of his sufferings by saying: "Thou tellest my wanderings: put thou my tears into thy bottle: are they not in thy book?" (verse 8)

When in Isaiah God remonstrates with the people for their sinfulness, He says of their disobedience, "Behold, it is written before me . . . " (Isaiah 65:6) And when in Malachi He promises hope for the faithful, the prophecy is worded:

> Then they that feared the Lord spake often one to another: and the Lord hearkened, and heard it, and a book of remembrance was written before him for them that feared the Lord, and that thought upon his name. Malachi 3:16

Finally, in the great prophecy of John's Revelation we read:

> And I saw the dead, small and great, stand before God; and the books were opened: and another book was opened, which is the book of life: and the dead were judged out of those things which were written in the books, according to their works. Revelation 20:12

Could the Cayce readings and the Bible be referring to the same unseen record? The very fact that the biblical text so consistently uses images related to books and writing suggests that the record is something other than the memory that would exist solely within the mind of God. If the passages given above were intended to speak only of God's memory, why did they go to such trouble to paint the image of something external to God, like a book? It would seem far more likely that these verses are indeed references to the very same "records" of which Edgar Cayce spoke.

If such records do exist, and if it is theoretically possible for the unconscious mind to communicate with other minds, we can see that it is not necessary to explain all psychic functioning in terms of mediumistic activity. Given the evidence we have considered, then, it does not seem unreasonable to conclude that the source of Edgar Cayce's information was not one forbidden in the Bible.

The 100 Percent Accuracy Criterion

Finally, in measuring Edgar Cayce as a psychic source, some comment concerning the "100 percent accuracy" criterion is in order. This criterion, which is invoked by many Christians in evaluating psychic sources, is based on a passage in Deuteronomy which says:

> But the prophet, which shall presume to speak a word in my name, which I have not commanded him to speak, or that shall speak in the name of other gods, even that prophet shall die.
> And if thou say in thine heart, How shall we know the word which the Lord hath not spoken?
> When a prophet speaketh in the name of the Lord, if the thing follow not, nor come to pass, that

is the thing which the Lord hath not spoken, but the prophet hath spoken it presumptuously: thou shalt not be afraid of him. Deuteronomy 18:20-22

On the strength of the last verse above, some fundamental Christians have suggested that one test of a modern-day psychic is whether he or she is always accurate. This test, of course, is one that all modern psychics are doomed to fail, for none could boast such an accuracy record. It is no secret that Edgar Cayce was not 100 percent accurate; the records of his readings include those cases in which he was wrong as well as those in which he was right, and no responsible representative of the Cayce material would claim 100 percent accuracy for these readings. On the basis of this fact alone, then, some fundamental Christians have suggested that Edgar Cayce fails a crucial test and, therefore, must have been a tool of the devil. But does this 100 percent accuracy criterion represent a valid application of the Deuteronomy passage?

We should note first that this passage applies to prophets who are claiming to be direct spokesmen for God. There is no evidence that Cayce ever made such a claim; to the contrary, both the conscious Cayce and his readings repeatedly admonished people not to take the content of this psychic material on authority, but rather to weigh it and test it to see if it is valid. Thus, we do not see Cayce presuming to speak a word in God's name.

Secondly, there is good biblical ground for questioning whether this passage was intended to establish the 100 percent accuracy criterion as it is often applied today. If the establishment of such an ironclad rule was the intention of the Deuteronomy passage, how do we explain the old favorite Bible story about Jonah? To summarize the essence of the story as it is told in the brief book of Jonah, the Lord instructs Jonah to go to the sinful city of Nineveh to "cry against" their wickedness. For reasons that are not entirely clear, Jonah is afraid or reluctant to fulfill this request, and so he attempts to escape God's notice by boarding a seagoing vessel. The Lord sends a terrible tempest to shake the reluctant prophet out of hiding, and, interestingly enough, the ship's crew figure out who is the cause of the great storm by casting lots. When the lots fall to Jonah, the crew know he is the cause of their danger and coerce him to confess the reasons behind his fleeing to their ship. Once Jonah is found out, they throw him overboard to rid themselves of the danger they believe he represents. It is then that the "great fish" swallows Jonah, who eventually repents of his unwillingness to obey God and is spit out on the dry land. Finally, at God's second bidding, Jonah goes to Nineveh and tells them, "Yet forty days, and Nineveh shall be overthrown." (Jonah 3:4)

Now there is an unexpected turn of events in this story. The people believe the word of God as spoken through Jonah and they repent. Then, to Jonah's utter dismay, the city is not destroyed, but spared because of the people's repentance. We are told that this "displeased Jonah exceedingly, and he was very angry." (Jonah 4:1) God had allowed Jonah's prophecy to be made incorrect.

We may see all kinds of explanations behind the "failure" of Jonah's prophecy, not the least of which being God's mercy. But that cannot change the fact that Jonah made a prophecy that "did not come to pass." According to the 100 percent accuracy criterion, we would have to conclude that Jonah had spoken "presumptuously." Yet we know from this prophet's harrowing tale that it was only after much prodding that God induced him to give this prophecy that ultimately did not come to pass. How can we say, then, that the passage in Deuteronomy gives us a hard-and-fast, cut-and-dried criterion for deciding which prophets are of God? It would seem more consistent with the *whole* of the biblical text to take this as a reference to the prophet's veracity in general.

For the biblically centered Christian, of course, that veracity must be determined on the basis of more than a psychic's accuracy rate. Ultimately, the question of veracity will have to do with the kind of information a psychic gives on doctrinal matters. It is this issue that we will consider next, as we go on to examine the Edgar Cayce information from a doctrinal standpoint in the next chapter.

10

Measuring Cayce Against
Core Christian Doctrines

I HAVE PRESENTED the evidence in support of the
position that both Edgar Cayce's spiritual integrity and
the nature of his psychic gift pass the tests suggested in
the biblical text. Now I must leave it to each reader to
consider the validity of this evidence in the light of his or
her own faith. Yet, while acknowledging that this decision is a personal matter that no argument can decide
definitively, I would like to proceed to the next step and
consider the readings of Edgar Cayce in the light of the
third major biblical criterion: Does the content of these
readings lead one toward, or away from, the God of the
Bible?

Now this question can be a bit more tricky than it might seem on the surface, for many doctrinally conservative Christians will not recognize subjective experience as evidence that one is being drawn toward God. This can be one of the bases of misunderstanding when the Cayce enthusiast attempts to defend the God-centered character of the readings. Many people who have found help in the Cayce readings and who believe that the message in this material has helped them find a living relationship with their God will state unequivocally that the Cayce material directs people toward God. They will point toward the richness of their prayer and meditation lives, and possibly even to a return to the church, as evidence of this positive influence from the Cayce readings. Certainly, from the perspective of many who have found such help in the readings, these results are evidence enough that Edgar Cayce leads people to grow in their relationship with God. Understandably, then, it is frustrating and even a bit insulting to have the reality of that relationship with God challenged. Yet if we can pause a moment and consider the reasoning behind these challenges from some Christian quarters, we are in a much better position to respond to them effectively.

Thinking back to the Satanic counterfeit theory discussed in chapter 7, we find the reasons behind many Christians' basic distrust of personal experience as a means of evaluating religious experience. *Given their underlying premise that deception is possible in personal experience,* we can see why, from this perspective, an external, authoritative source such as the Bible must be the ultimate measuring rod when it comes to deciding whether a given teaching moves one closer to, or further from, God. While any given student of the Cayce readings may or may not accept the underlying premise that deception may creep into one's religious experience, it *is* necessary that we work within this premise if we want to make a response that the more doctrinally conservative Christian can accept.

The ultimate test of the readings' compatibility with fundamental Christianity, after all, is whether such a Christian can embrace these readings *without* giving up essential elements of his or her faith. Therefore, when some Christians assert that Edgar Cayce denies, twists, or subverts doctrines that they hold to be fundamental *biblical* doctrines, there is only one way to respond: We must examine the Cayce readings relative to those doctrines and see just how they compare to these core aspects of conservative Christian belief. While it is not possible to anticipate every doctrine that may be brought up by such Christians for consideration, we can at least take a look at the ones most often mentioned in Christian literature that is critical of Cayce.

In order to address these doctrinal questions as concisely as possible, the remaining segments of this chapter are presented in a discontinuous question-and-answer format that will cover miscellaneous core Christian beliefs. Discussion concerning doctrines specifically related to Jesus will be reserved for chapter 11, where we will make a detailed examination of Cayce's readings concerning the person and work of Jesus Christ.

What Did Edgar Cayce Say About the Nature of God?

Some of the anti-Cayce literature has suggested that the God of the Cayce readings is not the personal God of the Bible, but merely an impersonal, universal "force." It is not hard to see where this notion comes from, for there are countless readings that refer to God as "Creative Force" or "Creative Forces." Some critics have even taken the latter plural form to be an indication that the readings of Cayce were polytheistic. But when we consider these appellations without taking into account some of the other Cayce readings about God, we really do not get the entire picture as it is presented in this material. For the readings that refer to God as "Creative Force" are matched and even outnumbered by those that refer to Him as the most personal and loving of parents.

As the reading excerpt below indicates, God the loving parent is alive and well in the Cayce material. I have selected this particular excerpt from among thousands like it because it is taken from a reading that was given as advice to those who were to set the projects and purposes of the Association for Research and Enlightenment, Inc. Thus we may see the following as a policy statement for all of the Association's work with the Cayce readings:

> The startling thing to every soul is to awaken to the realization that it is indeed a child of God! That is startling enough for any man, any woman, any being, in this sin-sick world!
>
> And yet it is the heritage of every soul to awake to the consciousness that God indeed is mindful of the children of men, and calls ever, "If ye will be my children, I will be thy God."
>
> This is the message, then, that you shall carry; for there is a loving Father that cares. That is thy message!
>
> There *is;* for you have experienced it, you can and you may experience it in your *own* life!
>
> Can anything, any experience, any condition be more worth while? That, though there are those things that make men afraid, there are turmoils in this or that direction in the relationships of human experience that may terrify thee for the moment, there is *He* who cares! And He may walk and talk with *thee!* 254-95

We are on firm ground, then, when we assert that the God of the Cayce readings is a personal, loving parent. But the God of the Cayce readings is also the limitless, creative power behind this universe. As such, the name "Creative Force" is equally appropriate for Him. Both descriptions are in keeping with the Lord God Jehovah of the Bible, for together they remind us that our Father-Mother God is indeed God of all that is.

Do the Cayce Readings Deny the Trinity?

Some Christian writers have charged that the readings of Edgar Cayce deny the doctrine of the Trinity. Possibly this misunderstanding is based on a casual reading of the many readings which refer to the "trinity" of body, mind, and soul within man. This concept by itself could easily appear to be a subversion of the doctrine of the Godhead's Trinity. But on closer reading we find that, far from substituting the body-mind-soul trinity for the Father-Son-Holy Ghost Trinity, the readings point to various trinities in this world as a reflection of the ultimate nature of the Godhead. For example:

> For as ye are in body, mind and soul one, so is the Father, the Son and the Holy Spirit one. 2282-1

> Just as you know from your spiritual interpretations, and from that you have been taught, the Father, the Son and the Holy Spirit are One; so are your body, mind and soul one. 1597-1

> Know, O son, that all stand as *one* with Him, who is the Creator and Maker of the heavens and the earth! and that all those things in nature which are manifestations before the children of men are *one* in their interpretations, in their understanding! and

that Life itself is a manifestation of God from the minutest creation to man himself! yea, that the music, the song of the spheres are as One! and Life itself is the manifestation of that Spirit of Creative Forces that makes each entity, each soul a portion of the Whole yet *with* the ability—through the gift of the Father—to know itself to be itself yet one with the Father.

Even as the Father, the Son, the Holy Spirit are one—so are Patience, Time and Space—so are Body, Mind and Soul one in Man. 1529-1

In the last excerpt, we see particular emphasis on the ways God's creations reflect Him. Unity yet diversity, oneness yet individuality are themes repeatedly played upon. Then the ultimate example of this paradox of one-ness-yet-individuality is given in the example of the Trinity, where Father, Son, and Holy Spirit are one.

What Is the Readings' Position on Heaven and Hell?

The concepts of heaven and hell are often a subject of debate. Even among the various Christian denominations we find considerable disagreement as to whether such places are real or allegorical. But for the fundamental Christian, heaven and hell, as described in the Bible, are very real indeed. Can we find room in the Cayce readings for a belief in heaven and hell? While it must be emphasized that different students may have different understandings of those readings, I believe that a Christian can find in the Cayce information concepts of heaven and hell that are consistent with the teachings of Scripture. The readings define them in this way:

On heaven: . . . "I have not yet ascended to my

Father" would to some indicate that the heaven and the Father are somewhere else—a place of abode, the center about which all universal forces, all energies must turn or give off from. Hence "up" may be rather from within, or to the within—of which each soul is to become aware. For heaven is that place, that awareness where the soul—with all its attributes, its Mind, its Body—becomes aware of being in the presence of the Creative Forces, or one with same. That is heaven. 262-88

Can we unravel this reading to get a definitive statement about the nature of heaven? We do see heaven defined as being in the presence of God and being united (or one) with Him. We also see an interesting analysis of the spatial concept of heaven. For the reading seems to suggest that heaven is a part of this physical universe insofar as it is the source of all energy and all creation. It even suggests that a soul's "body" can in some way inhabit heaven. Yet the notion that the direction of heaven is "up" is replaced with the notion that it is to be found within.

I will leave it to each reader to determine for himself or herself whether such a description of heaven is compatible with the biblical one. For me, readings like the one above echo Jesus' own statement that the kingdom of heaven is within. The idea that it is not to be found as a concrete place in this physical world makes it no less real. (For implications related to heaven and the bodily resurrection, see chapter 14.)

On hell: For the *law* is set—and it happens! though a soul may will itself *never* to reincarnate, but must burn and burn and burn—or suffer and suffer and suffer! For, the heaven and hell is built by the soul! The companionship in God is being one

with Him; and the gift of God is being conscious of
being one with Him, yet apart from Him—or one
with, yet apart from, the Whole. 5753-1

Leaving the obvious allusion to reincarnation aside
for the moment (for we will go into depth concerning
the question of reincarnation in Part Four), from this excerpt we can get an understanding of how the Cayce
material deals with the concept of hellfire. By defining it
as the "burning" and suffering that the soul goes through
when it chooses not to learn the lessons that life has to
offer, these readings stress hell as separation from (or
lack of communion with) God.

The suggestion that the soul burns and suffers when
it wills not to reincarnate offers an interesting perspective not only on hell but also on one of the common objections traditional Christians express concerning
reincarnation: If we have all kinds of chances and many
lifetimes to get right with God, why be in any hurry about
it, some Christians will ask? Doesn't reincarnation encourage us to be spiritual procrastinators? The emphasis the reading above places on the suffering such
procrastination involves should make one think twice
about reincarnation as an excuse to postpone obedience
to God. It should also be cause to reconsider the underlying assumption implied by such thinking. After all,
when someone is not in a hurry to get right with god,
thinking there are lots of lifetimes to do it, what does that
say about this person's concept of God's laws? That God's
will is an unpleasant drudgery to be done, rather than
the perfect law that makes for harmony and optimum
happiness in this life?

In contrast, the message of the reading under consideration is that we suffer hell and separation from God
when we choose to defy His will. By implication, peace and
happiness are to be found in compliance with God's will.

Still, some readers may be thinking, this "hell" that the soul makes for itself by resisting God's law is hardly the same thing as the final, eternal hell of the Bible. Indeed, some readers interpret Cayce to say that all souls will eventually make it to heaven, thus contradicting the fundamental Christian doctrine that some souls will be eternally lost. Yet while it is true that the Cayce readings emphasize the unfailing mercy of God and His willingness that no soul perish, do they in fact tell us there is any guarantee that all souls *will* be saved?

Do the Readings Promise Universal Salvation? Let's let the readings speak for themselves on this question:

(Q) Is it the destiny of every spiritual entity to eventually become one with God?

(A) Unless that entity wills its banishment. As is given with man, in the giving of the soul, the will, wherewith to manifest in the entity, whether spiritual, whether material. With that, the entity, either spiritual or physical, may banish itself. Again a compliance with law; as has been given, Hell [was] prepared for Satan and his angels, yet God has not *willed* that *any* soul should perish. Giving of will to His creation, Man, that man might be one with Him, giving man the privilege of exercising his (man's) will, or exercising His (God's) will to be one with Him. 900-20

It would seem, then, that the Cayce readings do not teach that all souls will be saved, in the sense of having eternal awareness of their individual identities, regardless of their choices. Rather it would seem that the soul has the freedom to choose "banishment." Just what is banishment? As we saw in the earlier excerpt elucidating the readings' concept of hell (5753-1), God's gift to us is the consciousness—the awareness—of being one with Him, yet "apart" from Him; that is, aware of ourselves as individuals, even as we experience the oneness. Banishment, in the context of the Cayce readings, suggests the loss of that capacity to know ourselves to be ourselves yet participate fully in the oneness. "Salvation" is the gift of being eternally in God's presence and having the individual consciousness with which to experience that oneness. While definitely stressing the mercy of God, the reading above reminds us that God has given us the free will to choose either self-will and banishment from Him, or God's will and oneness with Him. The acceptance of that gift is a matter of free will. It is clear from this excerpt that the readings of Edgar Cayce do not teach universal enjoyment of that condition wherein we are individual, yet one with God, irrespective of the choices we make. They *do* say, however, that it is not God who condemns us to loss of that condition, but the soul itself who has the free will to choose such banishment above conscious oneness with Him.

Is Edgar Cayce, Rather Than Jesus, the Center of the Readings' Philosophy?

Some Christian writers have charged that Cayce serves as a source of ultimate authority and even as an object of worship among those who are involved with his readings. Is this true? In one sense, I cannot answer for the millions of people who have been touched by Edgar Cayce's work. It is likely that there are some who have placed him on a pedestal. Undoubtedly, there are many who have given his readings more authority than those readings claim for themselves. It seems to be a part of human nature to seek heroes, whether they be movie stars, evangelists, or psychics. Yet, is it fair to hold those individuals responsible for the devotion they may receive, *if they have done nothing to encourage it?*

Certainly Edgar Cayce's readings did not encourage such elevation of themselves or of the man through whom they came. The A.R.E., in carrying on Cayce's work today, continues in this spirit by encouraging people to test the readings, rather than quote them as doctrine; offering lectures and publications by speakers and writers who are not necessarily in agreement with the readings; and encouraging a diversity of viewpoints when it comes to understanding the meaning of the readings.

It is from the readings themselves that this policy arises, for they consistently discouraged people from making Edgar Cayce the focal point in their spiritual lives. Consider the following excerpt from a Cayce reading. Its context is that he had just been asked for information about how to go about completing "A study of the phenomena as manifest through Edgar Cayce." This gentle but firm remonstrance came in reply:

These are very well, as it should be in others [other studies being asked about in that same reading?]. Study that rather as manifested through the Christ. Study what happened when the water turned to wine, what happened when He took her by the hand and lifted her up, what happened when He walked to His disciples upon the sea, what happened when He called Lazarus, what happened in the garden when His disciples—even His closest friends—slept while He fought with self; what happened on the Cross when He commended His mother to John, what happened when He spoke to Mary Magdalene; what happened when He spoke to Thomas, to the other disciples; what happened when He arose, "Go ye into all the world and preach the gospel." 262-100

Clearly the focus is on the life of Christ and all that that life entailed—from His ministry to His miracles to His resurrection and His final charge to spread the gospel throughout the world. When the sleeping Cayce is asked about himself, he responds by recommending that attention be placed on Christ instead. This does not sound like the words of a psychic who sought to usurp the role of Christ in people's spiritual lives. It sounds instead like the counsel of one who attempted to make people see beyond himself to the Christ. We see further evidence of this commitment to be Christ-centered, rather than Cayce-centered, in the readings that warn the A.R.E. not to become a cult.

Is the A.R.E. a Cult?

We often find the A.R.E. listed as a cult in Christian publications that seek to warn against such organizations and movements. What do these publications mean when they categorize the A.R.E. as a cult? Probably a variety of things, for "cult" is an interesting word that carries loaded connotations in our day. *Webster's New World Dictionary* defines a cult as "a system of religious worship or ritual; devoted attachment to, or extravagant admiration for, a person, principle, etc., especially when regarded as a fad; a group of followers; sect." Additional connotations today include images of mind control, mass psychology, and separation from traditional church, family, and community ties. Does the A.R.E. fit any of these definitions and connotations?

We can respond to the first of *Webster's* definitions by pointing out that there is no formalized worship or ritual in the A.R.E. Individuals are instead encouraged to seek the form of worship (with or without ritual) that best answers their needs. (More about the A.R.E. and the church in a moment.)

The second definition relates closely to the preceding discussion of Edgar Cayce as a central figure. Beyond the comments already made, I would point out that, though there are many principles expounded in the Cayce material, there is no effort to formulate these into a unified doctrine that may be shared by all A.R.E. members. The diversity of faiths among the A.R.E. membership is testimony to the organization's commitment to individual choice and responsibility in matters of religious faith. Even the perspective of this particular book, when seen in contrast to the other A.R.E. publications, is evidence that there is room for a wide range of beliefs and opinions among A.R.E. staff and members alike. Furthermore, the vast range of subject matter in the Cayce readings creates a natural climate of diversity. Some Cayce enthusiasts are very much involved with the health principles in the readings, for example, but do little or nothing with the spiritual. Some who are involved with the readings' philosophy do not work with the health concepts. Some who are fascinated with the ancient history covered in the Cayce material focus on that alone, and so on.

The circumstances described above serve equally well to guard the A.R.E. against becoming a "sect" with "followers." Such a heterogeneous group of people as the A.R.E. membership tends to defy classification under any one label. For these reasons, too, we find ample evidence against the use of mind control, mass psychology, or any tendency toward separation from normal social and sacred institutions. A.R.E. members and staff come from all social and economic strata. They live, work, and worship within their communities. They represent all levels of educational background. According to just about any criterion imaginable—positive or negative—students of the Edgar Cayce readings represent a cross section of the society in which they live.

This, too, is in keeping with the spirit of the readings, as the following excerpt illustrates:

> Hence the ideals and the purposes of the Association for Research & Enlightenment, Inc., are not to function as another cism or ism. Keep away from that! For these warnings have been given again and again. Less and less of personality, more and more of God and Christ in the dealings with the fellow man.
>
> To be sure, those phases of the activity of the Association, in the material plane, must take concrete evidence and present concrete evidence of its being grounded in mental and spiritual truth. But not that it is to build up any organization that is to be as a cism or a cult or ism, or to build up money or wealth or fame, or position, or an office that is to function in opposition with *any* already organized group.
>
> How did thy Master work? In the church, in the synagogue, in the field, in the lakes, upon the sands and the mountains, in the temple! And did He defy those? Did He set up anything different? Did He condemn the law even of the Roman, or the Jews, or the Essenes, or the Sadducees, or any of the cults or isms of the day? All, He gave, are as *one*—under the laws! And grudges, cisms, isms, cults, must become as naught; that thy Guide, thy Way, thy Master, yea even Christ—as manifested in Jesus of Nazareth—may be made known to thy fellow man! 254-92

The insistence that people not turn the A.R.E. into a cult that substitutes for their church involvement is repeated often in the Edgar Cayce material. For example, one person asked how he could conduct himself so as to be in accord with his church and yet maintain his involvement with an A.R.E. study group. The answer suggested that as long as Christ was the focus of both activities there would be no conflict. It further advised:

> If they [group affiliations] are not such in their relationship as to make for the glorification of Him as the head of the church in self, as the head of truth in the earth, have nothing to do with groups. 555-1

Finally, the readings advised that when individuals did find irreconcilable conflicts between the readings and the teachings of their faith, they should reject that which would take them away from their faith:

> (Q) If there is no conflict in the teachings of the Roman Catholic Church and the belief in reincarnation, why is it that I cannot find a coordination between the two?
> (A) This depends, to be sure, upon the outlook. If this is not in keeping with that which answers within self, then reject any that would make for a difference in thy religious beliefs or tenets. 1089-8

Far from encouraging cultish devotion, we see the readings of Cayce consistently deflecting such tendencies. Even when asked, "Is there any indication of what church I should join and associate with?" the readings responded with:

> Remember, rather, the church is within self. As to the organization, choose that—not as a convenience for thee but where ye may serve the better, whatever its name—let it be thy life proclaiming Jesus, the Christ. 3342-1

Proclaiming Jesus the Christ

Throughout the sampling of readings quoted in this chapter, we have seen references to the centrality of Christ. Yet, there is still much to be said regarding the readings of Cayce and the traditional Christian view of Christ. In fact, what many would consider to be the three most important areas of Christian doctrine remain to be dealt with in our discussion of *Edgar Cayce and Christian Faith:* What do the readings really say about the person and work of Jesus Christ? How can one reconcile the Christian doctrine of salvation with the concept of reincarnation? What is the Edgar Cayce readings' view of the Bible itself?

We will address the first of these remaining three questions in the next chapter. The last two questions will be the focus of consideration in Parts Four and Five, respectively.

11

The Christology of
the Edgar Cayce Readings

THE CAYCE READINGS have much to say about Jesus.
We find these readings advising people to turn to Him,
to trust in Him, to follow His teachings, and to meet Him
in prayer. Even a casual leafing through the pages of the
Cayce transcripts will indicate that in this particular psychic material, Jesus is a central figure indeed. "What,
then, will you do with Jesus?" one readings asks. (254-
95)

But for some Christians, the question is rather, "What
has Edgar Cayce done with Jesus?" For, his frequent
mention of Jesus notwithstanding, we find objections to
Cayce's readings about Jesus Christ to be at the heart of

most Christians' criticism of this psychic source. Why is this? Simply because, for some Christians, it is not the number of times the readings talk about Jesus—or even the number of times they recommend Him to the spiritual seeker—that really counts. For the person of traditional Christian faith, the real question is not *whether* the readings speak of Jesus, but what those readings *say* about the person and work of Jesus Christ when they do talk about Him; that is, what do the Cayce readings say about Jesus' nature, and what do they say about His purpose and accomplishment here on earth?

Essentially, the answers to these questions concerning the person and work of Christ constitute the Christology of the Edgar Cayce readings—or their perspective on the study of Christ. In this chapter, we will examine that Christology in some detail, first looking at the readings on Christ in a general way and then focusing more specifically on some of the readings' more unusual perspectives on Christ and the problems those perspectives raise for some Christians. Finally, we will take a look at the readings concerning key events in the life of Jesus to see how these compare with the Bible version.

I will be excerpting from the readings extensively in this chapter, as I feel it is very important to let the readings speak for themselves as much as possible on this sensitive subject. By allowing verbatim readings to form the substance of this exploration, I hope to increase the chances that each reader will draw his or her conclusions from the readings themselves rather than from me.

The Mission of Christ

Let's begin at the beginning and consider first the readings' statements concerning the mission of Christ. What does this psychic information say about His purpose in coming to the earth? Why did He come and what did He accomplish by being here? Most important, how does that mission relate to us? The Cayce readings, which present Jesus as a great Teacher and the perfect example for us to follow in our own lives, have been well circulated in numerous publications. Certainly this aspect of Jesus is one on which the readings speak eloquently and is one which deserves attention in any study of Edgar Cayce and Christianity. We will, in fact, spend some time in chapter 14 considering Jesus' role as the perfect pattern of human conduct. But is this all the readings have to say concerning Jesus' mission? Hardly. As the excerpts below will indicate, we find in the readings of Edgar Cayce that Jesus, as "the way," is presented as a central and unique figure, Savior and Atoner for all of humankind.

Jesus as the Way. To give the fuller context of the reading quoted at the beginning of this chapter:

> What, then, will you do with Jesus?
> For He is the Way, He is the Light, He is the Hope, He *is* ready. Will you let Him into thy heart? or will you keep Him afar or apart? Will ye not eat of His body, of the bread of life? Drink from that fountain that He builds in the minds, the hearts, the souls of those that seek to know Him and His purposes with men, with the world! 254-95

This reading gives us clues to several aspects of Cayce's Christology. First, we may note the identification of Jesus with "the way and the light." Although those terms are not defined in this particular reading, we can at least see agreement with the language of the New Testament in describing Jesus. We also notice that the Jesus of this reading has an enduring personal identity, holding the capacity to enter one's heart and in some way change one's life. We note also that the element of choice is with us. The reading makes it clear that we must choose and allow the entrance of Jesus into our lives.

So far, it would seem that the Cayce view of Jesus is quite consistent with the biblical one. But, of course, we have only looked at one reading. Is this one typical of the Cayce view of Jesus? Looking to another excerpt for further insights we find:

> Take it to Jesus! He *is* thy answer. He is Life, Light and Immortality. He is Truth, and is thy elder brother. 1326-1

Once again we encounter the theme of aid coming to us through Jesus, whose role this time is defined in terms of His being "thy answer" and of His identification with immortality. We also find a further mention of the personal nature of Jesus' relationship with us when we see Him called the "elder brother." Certainly, no Christian would object to the linking of Jesus with immortality and "the answer," but what about this description of Him as "elder brother"? This label, which is often applied to Jesus in the readings of Edgar Cayce, seems to echo such Bible passages as:

> For both he that sanctifieth and they who are sanctified are all of one: for which cause he is not ashamed to call them brethren . . . Hebrews 2:11

> For whosoever shall do the will of my Father which is in heaven, the same is my brother, and sister and mother. Matthew 12:50

It would seem that there is nothing new or unorthodox, then, in this reference to Jesus as our elder brother. Still, the Cayce readings' respect for all world religions has led some Christians to believe that the "elder brother" of the Cayce material is not the same as the Bible's unique Son of God. Is this true?

Jesus Is Central and Unique. While it is true that the Edgar Cayce information does show respect for other great spiritual teachers, such as Mohammed, Buddha, and Confucius, these other teachers do not supplant Jesus in the readings' scheme of things. The relationship between Jesus and other spiritual teachers is perhaps best demonstrated in the following statement: "Others may point the way, but have they the virtue and understanding of Him who said, 'I am the way, the truth, and the life'?" (John 14:6; *A Search for God,* Book I, p. 57)

The concept of Jesus' uniqueness is underscored in readings like the following:

(Q) On which of the Masters of Wisdom should I meditate for spiritual guidance?
(A) There's only one Master. 3545-1

This admonition that we place no teacher or master above Jesus is extended to include even Jesus' greatest servants, as we see in the following reading which advises us to substitute no one for the Master Himself:

Then *who* is the bridegroom, and who is the bride? Thyself—thy Lord!
Trust not any other than Him. For as He gave, it was not that ye should come unto Peter nor to Paul, but "unto *me!* If ye will abide in *me,* I will come and abide with thee!" 1597-1

Here, along with the admonition to place our trust in no one other than Jesus, we once again find the personal relationship with Jesus stressed, this time in the assurance that He is accessible to each one who seeks Him. Nor is the Jesus of the Cayce readings merely a helpful spiritual master, for we find His role as intermediary between God and man given great emphasis. For example, one reading tells us that "God gave to the world the Son, His Son, that we through Him might have eternal life" and speaks of Jesus as "an advocate with the Father," calling Him "even thy Elder Brother, who has promised to meet thee within thine own temple . . . He changeth not . . . rely not upon others." (1857-2)

As this reading and others indicate, Edgar Cayce's Christology includes the concept that Jesus serves as humankind's advocate with the Father. In fact, not only is He an advocate: In this reading's suggestion that "through Him [we] might have eternal life," we can see His advocacy extending to the point of His being a Savior.

Jesus as Savior. We are used to hearing, in Evangelical circles, about Jesus as Savior. Indeed, the entire focus of evangelism is to get people to the point of accepting Jesus as their Savior. But it might come as a surprise to some Christians to learn that Edgar Cayce also spoke of Jesus as a Savior. For example:

> Lean upon that thou hast learned in thine understandings, in thine knowledge of the dealings of the Father through the Son to the children of men! For His promises are sure . . .
>
> But in thy mental meditation, seek the Lord while He may be found. Put Him not away from thee, but seek *only* in the *name* of the *Christ,* the *Lord,* the *Son of Man!* the *Savior of the world!*
>
> And ye shall *know* the way, and the Way shall be in Him—and much good will come to thee through those very experiences that have made thee afraid. 1089-2

The readings of Edgar Cayce did not hedge on this concept of Jesus being Savior, for in another place they boldly assert:

> Isn't it a scientific fact that He is the savior of the world? . . . from the very first of the Old Testament to the very last even of Revelation, He is not merely the subject of the book, He is the author in the greater part, having given to man the mind and the purpose for its having been put in print. For it is in Him ye live and move and have thy being and as He gave, "Search ye the Scriptures, for they be they that testify of me, and in them ye *think* ye have eternal life."
> . . . For He is the beginning and the end of all things. 5322-1

Still, the skeptical or cautious Christian may want to know more about the *concept behind* this word *Savior* before concluding that the Cayce readings speak of Jesus in a way that is consistent with Scripture. Just how is it that Jesus saves us? For unless we can find room in the Cayce material for the doctrine of salvation through Jesus' atonement, an essential ingredient for the fundamental Christian has been left out.

Jesus as Atoner. The readings of Edgar Cayce are well known for breaking the word *atonement* down into syllables so that it is read as "at-one-ment." This tends to arouse suspicion in those who believe that Jesus' blood atonement on the cross was the apex of His saving mission here on earth. When Cayce uses the term *at-one-ment,* is this just a clever metaphysical substitute for the biblical doctrine of atonement, planned perhaps by Satan himself to throw us off the track and make us think the Cayce readings are Christ-centered? Such is the concern of some fundamental Christians who are not com-

fortable with this use of the word *atonement.* Or is it instead that Edgar Cayce gives this syllabic emphasis to
"at-one-ment" merely to show the *result* (reunion—or
at-one-ment—with God) of the atonement made by
Christ? Evidence from the readings themselves indicates
the latter to be the case, for we find both atonement and
at-one-ment used, and where reference is made to atoning, it seems very much in line with the biblical view:

> As given, without the shedding of blood there
> was no remission of sin . . .
> Hence the shedding of blood in the *man* Jesus
> made for the atoning for *all* men, through making
> Himself in at-onement with the law and with love.
> For, through *love* was brought the desire to make
> self and His brother in at-onement. Hence in the
> atoning or shedding of the blood comes the re-
> demption to man, through that which may make
> for *his*—man's—at-onement with Him. 262-45

It would seem fair, then, to interpret this reading as
saying that it is the atonement that makes at-one-ment
possible. Furthermore, we see much that is in accord
with the traditional Christian belief that the atonement
was made in the shedding of Jesus' blood in our behalf.

So far, so good. We find that the Jesus of the Cayce
readings is central, unique, and personal. We find further that though He is the Son of God, He is also our elder brother and advocate with the Father. His advocacy
extends to the point of His being no less than the Savior
of the world who made atonement for all humankind by
the shedding of His blood. Keeping in mind that we have
yet to consider how such an atoning work on Jesus' part
could mesh with the reincarnation philosophy that also
appears in the Cayce readings, can we imagine a Christology more in keeping with the biblical Jesus? Yet there *are*

still some problems, and lest it appear that I'm hiding something in not bringing them up, let's consider two less orthodox perspectives that the readings of Edgar Cayce offer on the person or nature of Jesus.

The Nature of Christ

Most Christian objection to Edgar Cayce's readings on Jesus can be traced to two factors: The readings which seem to separate Jesus and the Christ, and the readings which suggest that the being we know as Jesus had several incarnations before His culminating appearance as Jesus of Nazareth. Not surprisingly, these readings raise extremely important questions for any Christian who is evaluating the compatibility of Edgar Cayce with his or her faith. For, no matter how many times Edgar Cayce calls Jesus the Son of God, the Savior—even the Atoner—*is* there any way that one of Christian faith can sanction a psychic source that not only separates Jesus from Christ but tells us that this soul experienced other earthly incarnations? It is no exaggeration to say that, for many people of traditional Christian belief, such notions go beyond the merely errant to enter the category of truly blasphemous doctrines. Certainly, therefore, anyone hoping to bridge the Cayce readings with more traditional Christian belief should recognize and be sensitive to the immensity of the issues raised when we suggest these things about Jesus.

In my own experience with the Edgar Cayce material, the readings which suggest that Jesus had former lifetimes were the ones over which I did the most praying and Bible study. Any information that undermined Jesus' divinity or His unique role as the Son of God who sacrificed Himself for me would not have been acceptable. It was essential to me that I determine whether *all* of the readings about Jesus were compatible with my faith. I was prepared to have nothing more to do with Edgar Cayce if his readings could not be seen in a way that upheld what I believed to be essential Christian doctrines concerning Jesus' divinity and His sacrifice on our behalf.

It should probably be stressed here that these criteria, while essential for me, were matters related to my personal faith. Someone coming to the Cayce readings from a different perspective might not establish the same criteria for acceptance, and so I wish to emphasize that I am not attempting to codify "A.R.E. doctrine" concerning Jesus. I can only speak as one person of Christian belief, looking at the Cayce readings from that perspective, yet respecting the diversity of faiths that the A.R.E. encourages. (See the segment, "Is the A.R.E. a Cult?" in chapter 10.) For I have found the A.R.E., as a membership organization that does not promote any one religious doctrine, to provide a climate where the faith of one's choice can grow strong. We might find an analogy in the religious freedom we enjoy here in the United States. Is there any question but that Christianity is allowed to prosper here precisely because other faiths are allowed to prosper as well? Therefore, I leave it to the fundamental churches to promote the singular "rightness" of certain doctrines concerning Jesus and confine my own comments to those that show how Christianity is one belief system among many that may be seen as compatible with the readings of Edgar Cayce. It is in this spirit that I share the understanding I have come to hold with respect to the readings about Jesus.

As I considered the readings on Jesus' prior incarnations in the light of my beliefs and as I prayed for guidance concerning their truth or falsehood, I received what has been for me an answer to my questions. I do not claim that every seeker will find the same answer; indeed, I know that many students of the Cayce readings have a different understanding of the readings on Jesus than the one I am about to share. But I believe the explanation I offer here is one that shows how Jesus could be the unique, perfect Son of God who made atonement for all humankind and yet still have had prior incarnations in the earth. The understanding that I will be sharing here might not be the only possible view of the readings on Jesus, but it is one that a Christian might take without compromising essential elements of his or her faith.

"Jesus" vs. "Christ." When the Cayce readings separate Jesus and Christ, does that necessarily suggest a departure from what Scripture teaches about these two names? Let's take a look at the reading that is usually the source of this controversy and examine just what it says:

> (Q) Why do I have a leaning more towards Christianity than Judaism?
> (A) Hast thou not tried both? Has thou not found that the *essence,* the truth, the *real* truth is *one?* Mercy and justice; peace and harmony. For without Moses and his leader Joshua (that was bodily Jesus) there *is* no Christ. *Christ* is not a man! *Jesus* was the man; Christ the messenger; Christ in all ages, Jesus in one, Joshua in another, Melchizedek in another; *these* be those that led Judaism! These be they that came as that child of promise, as to the children of promise; and the promise is in thee, that ye lead as He has given thee, "Feed my sheep." 991-1

Leaving aside for just a moment the obvious references to Jesus' prior incarnations as Joshua and Melchizedek, what can we make of this statement that "*Christ* is not a man! *Jesus* was the man"? Must we take this to mean, as some have interpreted it, that Christhood was something apart from the man Jesus? That Jesus was a man who simply attained or manifested the attributes of Christhood? Under this interpretation, Christhood would not be seen as an inherent part of Jesus' makeup, but rather as something He achieved—like an advanced degree. While this is certainly the way many people understand the reading above, such an explanation is not compatible with the Christology of the fundamental Christian. Is there any alternative? For me, there is.

When we consider that "Christ" is simply the Greek version of the word *Messiah* or "anointed one," we can see another reason why the Cayce readings might have drawn a distinction between "Christ" and "Jesus." The concept, the *role,* of Messiah was one that had been planned for and prophesied for thousands of years before Jesus of Nazareth was born on this earth. People had some understanding of the role of Messiah long before it was linked for them with the specific identity of the man Jesus. Thus, "Jesus the Christ," "Jesus the Messiah" are ways of identifying the man with His office or mission.

The reading under consideration seems to make this same point when it says, " . . . without Moses and his leader Joshua . . .there *is* no Christ . . . Christ in all ages, Jesus in one . . ." (991-1) As any Bible student will know, the coming of Jesus Christ was an historical event; that is, it was linked to a long line of biblical prophecies and plans that culminated in the appearance of the Anointed One on earth. Thus, it is accurate to say that the Christ was in all ages, whereas Jesus of Nazareth—as a human identity—walked this earth in one particular age.

Now, when we recognize that the word *Christ* does not *mean* the same thing as the name *Jesus,* we are not necessarily saying that Jesus and Christ cannot be combined into a single identity. By analogy, we might call George Washington the first president of the United States. The "first president of the United States" is a particular office or role. George Washington was the individual identity who filled that role. But when we distinguish between "first president" as a role and "George Washington" as an individual's name, we do not mean to imply that "first president" and "George Washington" were not the same person. We are just recognizing two different designations—each with its own meaning—for the same individual.

I realize that the more theoretical question—could someone else have been the first president?—is yet to be addressed, for if Jesus just "happened" to be the Christ or Anointed One and any other soul could have theoretically "attained" that same office, we still have a problem. For fundamental Christian belief in the *eternal* deity and uniqueness of the single entity, Jesus Christ, is contradicted in any interpretations that see Christhood as a kind of ultimate attainment which the soul we know as Jesus was first to achieve. Again, while recognizing that many people do interpret the readings on Jesus in just this way, we can ask if that is the *only* possible interpretation. Is there another way of understanding the readings that is more compatible with fundamental Christianity? For me, there has been another way of understanding the circumstances under which Jesus "became" the Christ.

The Christ lived the complete earthly experience in order to free us from its bonds. In order fully to appreciate Jesus' Christhood, we must consider the momentous act of God becoming human. The entire Gospel is the story of how God became human in order to save us. Somehow, it seems, it was necessary for the Savior to join the human race before He could save the human race. The more deeply we ponder the paradox of God becoming human, the deeper the mystery becomes. One Cayce reading explains that He took on human form in order "to wipe away in the experience of man that which separates him from his Maker," and that He "in suffering the death on the Cross became the whole, the entire way; *the* way, *the* life, *the* understanding, that we who believe on Him may, too, have the everlasting life." (5749-6)

Just what does this mean? It might suggest that Jesus voluntarily took on the totality of human experience in order to lift us up from it. In other words, from the very beginning, the Christ entered the cycle of earthly incarnations for the sole purpose of redeeming us. His entry was wrapped up in the necessity of God becoming human in order to save us: He experienced our condition in order to make atonement for us, and in so doing He made the way of salvation complete.

Is there any basis for such an interpretation of the Cayce readings? And, more important by far, does such an interpretation adequately deal with the biblical data concerning Jesus? Let's identify the assumptions behind this interpretation of the Christ's incarnations and consider them one by one.

Assumption 1: The Edgar Cayce readings concur with the biblical doctrine that Jesus' ultimate sacrifice on the cross was for our benefit. The concept of a vicarious atonement is at the heart of fundamental Christianity; that is, Jesus' sacrifice on the cross was for our benefit. What does Edgar Cayce say about this?

> For His heart ached, yea His body was sore and weary; yea His body bled not only from the nail prints in His hands and feet but from the spear thrust into the heart of hearts! For the blood as of the perfect man was shed, not by reason of Himself but that there might be made an offering once for all . . . 1504-1

Assumption 2: The Christ's entry into a series of in-

carnations prior to His appearance as Jesus of Nazareth was for the purpose of rescuing us. Was Jesus at one time a lost soul just like the rest of us, or has His experience in the earth and even His reason for entering the earth in the first place been qualitatively different from ours? There is evidence in the readings supporting the understanding that He entered with the intention of redeeming us:

> For, did the Master Jesus come by chance? Or was it not according to the preparation made from the very foundations of the world? For as another has indicated, "Without Him there was not anything made that was made." 3645-1

This clear link of Jesus with the eternal Word (John 1:1-3) indicates that He is more than just a soul who attained perfection before other souls. He is instead represented as the eternal Son, whose mission of saving wayward souls was established at the very beginning of earthly existence.

Assumption 3: The act of making atonement for us entailed His taking on the vicissitudes of human experience. Is such a notion compatible with the message of Scripture concerning Jesus' atonement for us? Are there any biblical grounds for seeing redemptive intent behind the alleged incarnations of the Christ soul? Consider this passage from the Epistle to the Hebrews:

> But now we see not yet all things put under him [man].
> But we see Jesus, who was made a little lower than the angels for the suffering of death, crowned with glory and honour; that he by the grace of God should taste death for every man.

For it became him, for whom are all things, and by whom are all things, in bringing many sons unto glory, to make the captain of their salvation perfect through sufferings . . .

Forasmuch then as the children are partakers of flesh and blood, he also himself likewise took part of the same; that through death he might destroy him that had the power of death, that is, the devil . . .

For verily he took not on him the nature of angels; but he took on him the seed of Abraham.

Wherefore in all things it behooved him to be made like unto his brethren, that he might be a merciful and faithful high priest in things pertaining to God, to make reconciliation for the sins of the people.

For in that he himself hath suffered being tempted, he is able to succor them that are tempted. Hebrews 2:8b-10, 14, 16-18

While we cannot construe this passage to be making overt reference to Jesus having had prior lifetimes, we can see clear indications that experiencing our humanity was an important part of Jesus' redemptive work. We find a similar message in the Edgar Cayce readings:

For as has been given, He was tempted in all points like as we are, yet without error. Yet he bore in the body the sufferings of the body; want, loneliness—forsaken; and all that play upon the emotions of the bodily functions; knowing within self the abilities of self to by the mere word, by the speaking to the influences, eradicate these entirely. 1440-2

This reading places emphasis not only on Jesus' successful handling of the temptations put before Him in

His human experience, but also on His willingness to undergo hardships and limitations that He had the power to stop or prevent. Thus Jesus' full experience of humanity does not imply a lessening of His divinity but a voluntary compliance with the laws of this physical world. As it is stated in another reading:

> For, as given, the greatest service to God is service to His creatures; for, as shown in the Holy One, without spot or blemish, yet gave Himself that others through Him might have the advocate to the approach to the Father without fear; in that He had passed through the flesh and the rules of the earthly, fleshly existence, taking on all the weaknesses of the flesh, yet never abusing, never misusing, never misconstruing, never giving to others a wrong impression of the knowledge of the universe; never giving any save loving brotherhood . . . 254-17

We are reminded of that other passage in Hebrews which says that Jesus "was in all points tempted like as we are, yet without sin." (4:15)

Perhaps we have the ultimate biblical evidence that Jesus' mission involved taking on our condition when we are told of His crying out on the cross, "My God, my God, why hast thou forsaken me?" (Matthew 27:46) Although the Christ voluntarily entered earthly experience and could have at any time used His omnipotence to escape the sacrifice set before Him, He chose instead to take our separation from the Father on Himself. As one reading explained His final cry of despair on the cross:

> This came, as He promised, that that anguish, that despair may not be in thy experience. It was a fulfilling; that the trials, the temptations might be

shortened in the days of expression, that the very elect might not be disturbed in their search for Him. 2072-4

Assumption 4: Jesus' vicarious atonement for us was made complete in His taking our separation from the Father upon Himself. Another reading gives further insights concerning what happened as Jesus gave His life on the cross, when it describes this act as the fulfilling of the Law:

> On what wise, then, ye ask, did this [the fulfilling of the law] happen in materiality? Not only was He dead in body, but the soul was separated from that body. As all phases of man in the earth are made manifest, the physical body, the mental body, the soul body became as each dependent upon their own experience. Is it any wonder that the man cried, "My God, my God, *why* hast thou forsaken me?" 5749-6

This seems to be saying that Jesus took on the human condition so completely that the soul was separated from the body at the moment before His death. It also suggests that as He made vicarious atonement for us, the physical, mental, and soul experiences of humankind in the earth became His own burdens; that is, in order to rescue us from our separation from the Father, He took on all of the anguish of this separation. As the reading asks, is it any wonder that He felt forsaken in that moment of supreme sacrifice, for in that moment He took on our consciousness of being cut off from the Father?

When He overcame death of body and spirit on that first Easter morning, He made our rescue complete. In taking on our condition and then triumphing over it, He gave the same triumph to us. We find other Cayce readings which support the view that Jesus took on human conditions in order to free us from the spiritual bondage of those conditions:

> Then, be one—in thy purpose. Know, as given of old, the man called Jesus is the Savior of the world. He has purchased with His own will that right for direction. And He has promised, "I will never leave thee—I will not forsake thee," save that *thou*—as an individual—cast Him out, or reject Him, for counsel from some other source. 2970-1

> For as He, thy Master, thy Lord, thy Christ fulfilled the law by compliance with same, He became the law and thus thy Savior, thy Brother, thy Christ! 1662-1

> Remember rather the pattern as was manifested for thee in the Son; how that though He were the Son, yet learned He obedience through the things which He suffered.
> He used, then, that which was necessary in the experience in the earth as periods of suffering, as periods of rejection, even by His own that He had called, that were His friends; not as stumbling-stones but as steppingstones to make for thee, for the world, that access for each soul, for the closer relationship of the Father, through the Son, to the children of men. 2600-2

Assumption 5: The process of the Christ's taking on the human condition involved more than just the single incarnation as Jesus of Nazareth. Given the readings' indications that the Christ first entered the cycle of earthly incarnations for the purpose of rescuing us and considering the clear emphasis these readings place on

Jesus' taking on our condition in order to lift us from it, it seems reasonable to infer that not just His incarnation as Jesus of Nazareth but *all* of the Christ's earthly appearances were part of His redemptive work. This gives us a firm basis for the interpretation that regards Jesus as not merely the first soul among many to attain perfection, but as the eternal Son of God whose entire existence— both in this earth and out of it—has been devoted to rescuing wayward souls.

Examining These Assumptions in the Light of Scripture. Even if we can make a case for such a Christology being consistent with the readings of Edgar Cayce, are there any biblical grounds for this view of the Christ's work? We have already considered the information in Hebrews, chapter 2, which suggests that Jesus' effectiveness as a Savior was augmented by His taking on the human form and condition. Is there any further evidence that might allow us to go that extra step and entertain the notion that the Christ may have had several incarnations?

I make no claim that the Bible mentions any prior incarnations of Christ. My intention, rather, is to show that a belief which includes the notion that He made appearances in the earth prior to His incarnation as Jesus of Nazareth does not contradict what the Bible *does* say about Jesus Christ. Further, I hope to demonstrate that there is scriptural evidence to suggest that there are, in fact, some spiritual truths which, for various reasons, were not revealed during Jesus' ministry or in the course of the writing of the New Testament books.

Did Revelation Stop When the Bible Was Completed? I recognize that some Christians believe that in the closing words of the Book of Revelation we have a prohibition against further revelation:

> For I testify unto every man that heareth the
> words of the prophecy of this book, If any man shall
> add unto these things, God shall add unto him the
> plagues that are written in this book:
> And if any man shall take away from the words of
> the book of this prophecy, God shall take away his
> part out of the book of life, and out of the holy city,
> and from the things which are written in this book.
> 22:18, 19

These are stern warnings, and the consequences of ignoring them are stiff. But does this passage mean, as some have interpreted it, that all revelation was complete when the Bible was finished? Was this warning intended to apply to the whole of the Bible, or just to the book in which it appears? It seems more likely that the admonition not to add to or subtract from the book refers to John's Revelation, for John recorded his revelation as a book unto itself—not as the last chapter in an ongoing work. The New Testament as we know it today is a *collection* of books and letters that were written each within its own context, irrespective of the others. If they hang together as a unified revelation, it is due to the inspiration of the Holy Spirit and not because they were planned as a unit by the various writers. How can we take John's warning to apply to all future revelation, when he could not even have known that his would end as the last book of the Bible? Furthermore, we must deal with biblical prophecies that link the giving of prophecies with the last days. For example:

> And it shall come to pass afterward, that I will
> pour out my spirit upon all flesh; and your sons and
> your daughters shall prophesy, your old men shall
> dream dreams, your young men shall see
> visions . . . Joel 2:28

Thus the important question for us to consider is not whether the Bible allows for revelations to come after the Bible, but whether "revelations" such as Cayce's new perspective on Jesus are consistent with what the Bible has already revealed. Does the Bible reveal anything that is consistent with the Cayce readings' additional information about Jesus? It just might. For in several places it does seem to suggest that there is more to know about Jesus than what is overtly spelled out in Scripture. For example, in Jesus' last talk with His disciples He tells them:

> I have yet many things to say unto you, but ye cannot bear them now.
> Howbeit when he, the Spirit of truth, is come, he will guide you into all truth: for he shall not speak of himself; but whatsoever he shall hear, that shall he speak: and he will show you things to come.
> He shall glorify me: for he shall receive of mine, and shall show it unto you. John 16:12-14

This clear reference to the Holy Spirit's ability to bring additional revelations is sometimes seen as applying only to those disciples who were to go on and spread Jesus' teachings after His departure from this earth. Yet the New Testament contains accounts of the Holy Spirit being accessible to all believers. For example, the gifts of the Spirit, as they are enumerated in Paul's first letter to the Corinthians, include such abilities as "the word of wisdom," "the word of knowledge," "prophecy," and "discerning of spirits." (I Corinthians 12:8-10) This would suggest that new revelations or new understandings are not condemned by Scripture *so long as they do not contradict the biblical revelation that has gone before.*

The idea that there is room for growth in our understanding of certain aspects of Jesus Christ appears to be expressed quite clearly by the writer of Hebrews when he says, in discussing Jesus:

> Of whom we have many things to say, and hard to be uttered, seeing ye are dull of hearing.
> For when for the time ye ought to be teachers, ye have need that one teach you again which be the first principles of the oracles of God; and are become such as have need of milk, and not strong meat.
> For every one that useth milk is unskillful in the word of righteousness: for he is a babe.
> But strong meat belongeth to them that are of full age, even those who by reason of use have their senses exercised to discern both good and evil.
> Hebrews 5:11-14

This passage clearly indicates that not only is there more to be said than the writer feels comfortable revealing, but that the *nature* of what might be revealed is so sensitive that it could easily confuse or lead astray anyone whose ability to discern good and evil was not finely tuned. Thus, we have the hint of additional and potentially misconstruable information concerning Jesus. Let's explore the context of this passage more thoroughly.

A Brief Study of Hebrews 5-8. The context is essentially the same one we considered earlier in connection with the verses from the second chapter. The fifth chapter continues with a discussion of Jesus Christ as our intermediary with God, or "High Priest," as He is often called in this book. It draws a distinction between the Old Testament high priests, who made temple sacrifices not only for the people but for themselves as well, and Christ the perfect High Priest who is able to atone for us.

Continuing with verse five of the fifth chapter we read:

> So also Christ glorified not himself to be made an high priest; but he that said unto him, Thou art my Son, to-day have I begotten thee.
> As he saith also in another place, Thou art a priest for ever after the order of Melchisedec [sic]. Hebrews 5:5-6

Here we find at least a symbolic link between Jesus and the Old Testament figure, Melchizedek, whom the Cayce readings identify as one of the Christ's prior incarnations. More on that in a moment. For now, let's continue following the line of thought developed in Hebrews 5:

> Who [presumably referring to Jesus] in the days of his flesh, when he had offered up prayers and supplications with strong crying and tears unto him that was able to save him from death, and was heard in that he feared;
> Though he were a Son, yet learned he obedience by the things which he suffered;
> And being made perfect, he became the author of eternal salvation unto all them that obey him;
> Called of God an high priest after the order of Melchisedec [sic]. Hebrews 5:7-10

It is in this context, after this description of how Jesus "learned" obedience through suffering and then, being "made perfect," "became" the author of salvation, that we find the verse which suggests that there are "many things to say" of Him that are "hard to be uttered." For those who have a problem with Cayce references to Jesus "becoming" the Christ and to His having had a variety of human experiences, we might point out verse 9's refer-

ence to Jesus' being "made perfect." Given Hebrews' as-
sertion elsewhere that Jesus was tempted, yet without
sin (4:15), we must understand His being made "perfect"
in terms of His mission reaching completion, rather than
His faults being overcome. There is room to interpret the
Cayce readings in the same way, too, for they also speak
of His being perfect and without fault. (See readings
1504-1, 1440-2, 254-17, given on pp. 127, 129, 130, 199,
254, and 256.)

We find Jesus linked with Melchizedek once again in
the last verse of chapter 6, which tells us that Jesus is a
"forerunner" for us, who was "made an high priest for
ever after the order of Melchisedec." (verse 20) Chapter
7 then goes on to tell us some things that suggest
Melchizedek may not have been an ordinary man. Surely
the link between Melchizedek and Christ is strengthened
when we read:

> For this Melchisedec, king of Salem, priest of the
> most high God, who met Abraham returning from
> the slaughter of the kings, and blessed him;
> To whom also Abraham gave a tenth part of all;
> first being by interpretation King of righteousness,
> and after that also King of Salem, which is, King of
> peace;
> Without father, without mother, without descent,
> having neither beginning of days, nor end of life;
> but made like unto the Son of God; abideth a priest
> continually. Hebrews 7:1-3

Is it such a reach to infer from this biblical text that
Melchizedek and Jesus were two appearances of the
same Being? Who else can we imagine being without
beginning or ending of days and abiding a priest forever?
Even the titles, King of righteousness and King of peace
or Salem, match the labels usually reserved for Jesus.

Could the writer of Hebrews have made it any clearer if he had said, "Melchizedek and Jesus are the same Person"? And if we allow that the Christ could have made one prior appearance, is there any reason to rule out the possibility that He had several? Rather, it would seem in keeping with God's abiding concern for humanity that the Son should have periodically walked this earth until the "perfection" or culmination of His mission in the appearance as Jesus of Nazareth.

I realize that the suggestion that Christ may have appeared in the earth more than once is still foreign to many Christians. I certainly do not expect my explanation of how prior incarnations of Jesus might fit within the parameters of core Christian belief to make these readings on Christ acceptable to every Christian who reads them. Nor do I wish to give the impression that I advocate incorporating belief in the Christ's previous incarnations into the articles of Christian faith. I do maintain, however, that belief in these prior incarnations need not compromise belief in Jesus' eternal Godhood nor the vicarious nature of His sacrifice in taking on humanity and the death of the cross. If one is able to affirm those two tenets, then the most fundamental of Christian fundamentals remain unassailed. My personal stand, therefore, is that a person of traditional Christian belief need not see the more unusual aspects of Cayce's perspective on Jesus as damaging to Christian faith, even if he or she does not personally agree with them.

We have now considered the Cayce readings which reflect on both the mission and the nature of Jesus Christ. We have seen how some of these readings match traditional Christian doctrine and how others, though less traditional, may be interpreted in a way that is compatible with basic Christian faith. One more category of readings concerning Jesus should be considered before we leave our examination of the readings' Christology.

These are the readings which speak of circumstances in Jesus' life which today form important aspects of Christian belief concerning Him.

Edgar Cayce on the Life of Jesus

It is generally known that some of Edgar Cayce's readings fill in the gaps where the Bible is silent about circumstances surrounding the life of Jesus. While it is beyond the scope of this work to discuss these readings in detail, the specific places where Cayce readings on the life of Jesus interface with the biblical account are important to our discussion. For example, Cayce speaks at some length about the sect of Jews called Essenes, whom he says actively prepared for the coming of the promised Messiah. Of this preparation he says:

> *Ye* say that there were those periods when for four hundred years [the approximate time span between the close of the Old Testament and the opening narrative of the New] little or nothing had happened in the experience of man as a revelation from the Father, or from God, or from the sources of light. *What* was it, then, that made the setting for the place and for the entering in of that consciousness into the earth that *ye* know as the Son of man, the Jesus of Nazareth, the Christ on the Cross? Did the darkness bring the light? Did the wandering away from the thought of such [light] bring the Christ into the earth? Is this idea not rather refuting the common law that is present in spirit, mind and body that "Like begets like"? As was asked oft, "Can any good thing come out of Nazareth?" Isn't it rather that there were those, that ye hear little or nothing of in thine studies of same, that dedicated their lives, their minds, their bodies, to a purpose, to a *seeking*

for that which had been to them a promise of old? Were there not individuals, men and women, who dedicated their bodies that they might be channels through which such an influence, such a *body* might come? 262-61

Is the idea that a sect of people actively prepared for the coming of the Messiah consistent with Scripture? In the light of the Old Testament prophecies that foretold His coming and admonished the people to look for it, we might well expect just such a group. While at first we might wonder why, if the Essenes did play such a role, the Bible makes no mention of it, we can see that it was important for Jesus to be presented not as the property of one small sect, but as the Christ for all Judaism and all humankind. Other Cayce readings, which indicate that the adult Jesus was not a practicing Essene, suggest further reason for the Bible's silence on this sect's role.

On the birth of Jesus: In the story that unfolds in the Cayce readings, Mary and Joseph both had affiliation with the Essene group. Thus, the Cayce story of Jesus' birth fits within the biblical one. In fact, far from contradicting the Bible's account, the readings concur with Scripture's reports of all of the most miraculous circumstances surrounding the birth of Jesus: the angel's announcement to Mary, the star of Bethlehem, the heavenly choir, the Wise Men, are all discussed in moving detail. The virgin birth itself, often a subject of doubt even among fundamental Christians of some denominations, is upheld as fact. Even the Roman Catholic teaching that Mary was also without human father is affirmed in the readings which explain the virgin birth:

(Q) Was Anne prepared for her part in the drama as mother of Mary?

(A) Only as in the general, not as specific as Mary after Mary being pointed out [identified as the mother of the coming Messiah].

See, there was no belief in the fact that Anne proclaimed that the child [Mary] was without father. It's like many proclaiming today that the Master was immaculately conceived; they say "Impossible!" They say that it isn't in compliance with the natural law. It *is* a natural law, as has been indicated by the projection of mind into matter and thus making of itself a separation to become encased in same—as man did [in the beginning]. 5749-8

The reference above to the projection of mind into matter is an allusion to the coming of the human soul into physical form at the time of creation. Thus, we might paraphrase the reading to say that that which was possible when humans were created was certainly possible at the time of the incarnation of the Christ. If God could create humans in the first place, why would it be impossible for Him to create a child without a human father?

On the childhood of Jesus: From a close parallel with the biblical story of the birth and infancy of Jesus, the readings then go on to expand upon what is left uncovered by the Bible. A rather substantial gap in Jesus' biography is filled in by readings which suggest what He may have been doing during those biblically silent years, from the time after His appearance in the temple at age twelve to the beginning of His public ministry at age thirty. Cayce suggests that this was a period of intense study for Jesus, when He learned, among other things, about all of the major world religions.

While some might object that, as the perfect man, Jesus needed no instruction, such objections bear similarity to assertions that the infant Jesus would not have cried. In the very act of taking on human form, Christ elected to make Himself in some ways subject to the laws of human existence. It seems reasonable, then, to expect that as a boy and young man He underwent the normal stages of human development, mentally as well as physically. If it is said that He studied all of the world religions, that does not take away from the truth He carried within His very being, any more than the enrollment in a course in ethics would imply that one was not moral to begin with. Unless we wish to hold to the position that Jesus had *conscious* omniscience from the moment of His birth, it is not unreasonable to expect that He may have studied.

Returning to the central criterion that the readings of Edgar Cayce not contradict what the Bible *says*, we should note that these particular readings deal with a life period about which the Bible is silent. Therefore, there is little chance of contradiction.

On Jesus' ministry: We have already spent considerable time in this chapter exploring the readings' view of Jesus' mission; we will take the exploration even further in chapters 13 and 14, when we examine reincarnation in the light of that mission. But what about the events that made up the earthly ministry of Jesus Christ? Do the Cayce readings describe the same Jesus we read about in the Bible, or do they present a different account of Jesus' earthly ministry? In short, where do the Cayce readings stand with respect to the biblical Jesus?

It seems that, in every detail, this psychic account of Jesus' public ministry corresponds with what we find recorded in Scripture. From the wedding in Cana to the raising of Lazarus, from the gathering of the disciples to the encounter with Mary Magdalene, from the walking on the water to the healing of the ten lepers, and from the Sermon on the Mount to the Last Supper, the Cayce material presents an account that upholds the scriptural one. (See chapter 15 for additional discussion of the Last Supper and other Bible events.) In some areas the Cayce material does give additional information concerning family relationships, people's innermost responses to Jesus, and the results His ministry was to have during the rest of their lives. But nowhere do we find a Cayce account that is inconsistent with the biblical one. Right through Jesus' crucifixion, resurrection, and even His second coming, we find that the readings parallel the scriptural account.

On the resurrection: The resurrection of Jesus Christ stands out among the articles of Christian faith, not only as ultimate proof of His deity, but as evidence of His triumph over death. For the biblically centered Christian, belief in the resurrection is indispensable to Christian faith. What, then, do we find in the Cayce readings concerning this all-important event?

First, we find those readings which affirm the fact of the bodily resurrection. For reasons I cannot fathom, some Christian writers have charged that Edgar Cayce denies the bodily resurrection of Christ. Yet a study of the readings will reveal that this psychic spoke of the resurrection, not as metaphysical allegory, but as a literal event:

> [For in the] resurrection, here we find that in which ye *all* may glory. For without the fact of His overcoming death, the whole of the experience would have been as naught. 5749-10

> But when the Prince of Peace came into the earth for the completing of His *own* development in the earth [Can we tie this in to Hebrews' reference to His being "made perfect"?] *He* overcame the flesh

and temptation. So He became the first of those that overcame death in the body, [and this] enabl[ed] Him to so illuminate, to so revivify that body as to take it up again, even when those fluids of the body had been drained away by the nail holes in His hand[s] and by the spear piercing His side. 1152-1

Hence when those of His loved ones and those of His brethren came on that glad morning when the tidings had come to them, those that stood guard heard a fearful noise and saw a light, and—"the stone has been rolled away!" 5749-6

And, in gently admonishing some for their doubt, one Cayce reading asks:

Dost thou believe that He has risen? How spoke Thomas? "Until I see, until I have put my hand in his side where I saw water and blood gush forth, until I have handled his body, I will *not* believe." 5749-6

In each of these readings we can find affirmation of the bodily resurrection. In the first, we are told that without the resurrection, the whole point of Jesus' mission would have been lost. In the second excerpt, we have the graphic description of a body that was so certainly dead that its fluids were drained. Yet He "revivified" it. In the next excerpt we find reference to the stone being rolled away from the tomb—hardly the result of an allegorical resurrection! In the last reading, disbelief that He in fact arose is linked to Thomas, known throughout Christendom as one who inappropriately doubted. Can there be any question of the readings' position concerning the bodily resurrection?

Going beyond the affirmation of the fact of the resurrection, the readings speak of the significance of this great event when they describe the women's meeting with the angels in front of Christ's tomb on that first Easter morning:

> How, why, took they [the angels] on form? That there might be implanted into their [the women's] hearts and souls that *fulfillment* of those promises.
>
> What separates ye from seeing the Glory even of Him that walks with thee oft in the touch of a living hand, in the voice of those that would comfort and cheer? For He, thy Christ, is oft with thee. 5749-6

> There should be the reminding that—though He bowed under the burden of the Cross, though His blood was shed, though He entered into the tomb—through that power, that ability, that love as manifested in Himself among His fellow men He broke the bonds of death; proclaiming in that act that *there is no death* when the individual, the soul, has and does put its trust in Him. 5749-13

Finally, the meaning of the resurrection in one's personal life is brought out in this reading, which proclaims:

> . . . let it ever be said of thee that ye will make, ye will cause the welkin [sky] to ring for the glory of the coming of the Lord. For He will one day come again, and thou shalt see Him as He is, even as thou hast seen in thy early sojourns [a prior incarnation] the glory of the day of the triumphal entry and the day of the Crucifixion, and as ye also heard the angels proclaim "As ye have seen Him go, so will ye see Him come again." 3615-1

Thus in the Cayce readings the glory of the risen Lord

extends beyond even the triumph of the first Easter morning, for, in this material, Jesus Christ's coming again is joyfully predicted.

On the second coming: There is no more cherished hope among fundamental Christians than that they may live to see the return of the risen Christ. Though some Christian denominations interpret this event to be a figurative one, wherein the *spirit* of Christ will prevail in the earth, the more fundamental Christian awaits the *bodily* return of Jesus Christ to rule on this earth for 1,000 years. Where do the Cayce readings stand on this question? Do they speak of the second coming? And, if so, do they speak of it as a literal event or as a figurative one?

While there are certainly readings which speak of His coming into the hearts and minds of people, this form of His coming seems to be merely the precursor to the bodily return. For example:

> . . . what must be obliterated? Hate, prejudice, selfishness, backbiting, unkindness, anger, passion, and those things of the mire that are created in the activities of the sons of men.
>
> Then again He may come in body to claim His own . . . And He comes again in the hearts and souls and minds of those that seek to know His ways.
>
> These be hard to be understood by those in the flesh . . . yet those that call on Him will not go emptyhanded . . . 5749-5

Thus we see an indication that first He may come in spirit and then eventually He will come in the flesh. Concerning the timing of this second coming, the readings, like the Bible, tell us that no one knows exactly when it will be:

The time no one knows. Even as He gave, not

even the Son Himself. *Only* the Father. Not until His enemies—and the earth—are wholly in subjection to His will, His powers. 5749-2

This reading and others seem to suggest that the unpredictable timing of Jesus' second coming is tied up in the choices we make here on earth. It is we who, through our obedience to Him or lack of it, hasten or delay His return. For example, when one person asked about a specific date, he was told:

How doth He interpret, as to the day or the hour? No man knoweth save the Father.

Live ye then, each soul, as though ye expected Him today. Then ye shall see Him as He is, when ye live such a life. 3011-3

Here again we find the hint that Jesus may appear to individuals before a general, historical event that would be universally witnessed. In another reading, the possibility that He might appear to individuals prior to a universal appearance is explained in this way:

. . . all power in heaven, in earth, is given to Him who overcame. Hence He is of Himself in space, in the force that impels through faith, through belief, in the individual entity. As a Spirit Entity. Hence not in a body in the earth, but may come at will to him who *wills* to be one with, and acts in love to make same possible.

For, He shall come as ye have seen Him go, in the *body* He occupied in Galilee. The body that He formed, that was crucified on the cross . . . that appeared to Philip, that appeared to "I, even John." 5749-4

Thus, this reading affirms Christ's eventual return in His resurrected body. In the meantime, He may appear in spirit to those who look for Him. Such a possibility is an inspiration indeed! Perhaps the Cayce readings' message concerning the resurrection is best expressed in this reading, which advises that, though we do not know the specific time of His coming, it is near:

> Then, as that coming into the world in the second coming—for He will come again and receive His own, [those] who have prepared themselves through that belief in Him and acting in that manner; for the *Spirit* is abroad, and the time draws near, and there will be the reckoning of those even as in the first so in the last, and the last shall be first; for there is that Spirit abroad—He standeth near. He that hath eyes to see, let him see. He that hath ears to hear, let him hear that music of the coming of the Lord of this vineyard, and art *thou* ready to give account of that *thou* hast done with thine opportunity in the earth as the Sons of God, as the heirs and joint heirs of glory *with* the Son? Then make thine paths straight, for there must come an answering for what *thou* hast done with thine Lord! He will not tarry; for having overcome He shall appear even *as* the Lord *and* Master. Not as one born, but as one that returneth to His own, for He will walk and talk with men of every clime, and those that are faithful and just in their reckoning shall be caught up with Him to rule and to do *judgment* for a thousand years! 364-7

We can see, then, that the Cayce view of the second coming holds all of the promise that we read in the Bible itself. I can think of no better conclusion to these comments on the resurrection and to all of the foregoing comments on the Christology of the Cayce readings than this message given to one individual in her reading:

> Thou wilt be among those in the earth when He comes again. Glory in that, but let it be rather the one reason why ye keep the faith, the faith in the coming of the Lord, to call those who have been faithful; that they, as He prayed, "may be where I am, and may behold the glory which I had with thee before the worlds were."
>
> That is something to look forward to! . . .
>
> Though many of His children become wayward and far, far afield, He has not willed that any should perish but has left with the children of men, His brethren, that privilege of making those aware of this whose lives and hearts have only seen the hardships of the earth in man's mad desire for power in his material self. He has left it to those of the faithful to make such aware.
>
> Then know, as ye walk in the presence of the Master, it will be as leaning on the arm of someone to whom ye have pointed the way to the Christ-life— just as the beloved in the hour that there was set forth the emblem of the broken body and the shed blood, in order that man might ever be mindful of same—the beloved leaned upon the arm and the breast of His Lord. 3615-1

Part
Four

Reincarnation and Christian Faith

12

Getting Back to Definitions

NO MATTER HOW emphatically we may remind our critics that the Edgar Cayce readings contain no "teachings"—in the doctrinal sense—the fact remains that certain concepts *are* discussed repeatedly in this material. Nor can we deny that these concepts make up a general worldview or philosophy of living in which reincarnation plays a central role. Of course, we can point out—quite truthfully—that belief in reincarnation is not required for membership in A.R.E.; but this only skirts the issue, for most proponents of the Edgar Cayce material *do* seem to incorporate reincarnation into their personal belief systems.

We shouldn't be surprised, then, when some Christians fault the Cayce readings for "teaching" reincarnation. In one sense, they do "teach" it. The chances are fairly strong that an individual who is attracted to the readings of Edgar Cayce either holds a reincarnationist view already or will eventually develop one. So, regardless of whether the Cayce readings *cause* people to become reincarnationists, they do at the very least provide a framework in which the reincarnationist can be very comfortable. The important question, then, is whether belief in reincarnation is destructive to Christian faith; or, is it possible to be a reincarnationist and be committed to biblical Christianity at the same time? If not, then the biblically centered Christian has no alternative but to reject the readings of Edgar Cayce as promoting a philosophy that is destructive to Christian faith.

But if there is nothing inherently antibiblical in the reincarnation philosophy, then one of the chief obstacles to reconciliation of the Cayce readings with Christianity can be removed. In fact, if reincarnation and biblical Christianity *are* compatible, then a lot of good intentions on both sides are being wasted on unnecessary conflict. I believe that, when we strip away the misunderstandings, there is a surprisingly strong compatibility between reincarnation and the fundamentals of Christian faith. In the pages that follow, I will build my case for this conviction. Each reader will, of course, have to weigh the evidence in the light of his or her own faith.

If we are to iron out the differences between reincarnation and traditional Christianity, definitions are a very good place to begin. Defining terms may seem like a dull and even elementary step, but the importance of building this foundation should not be underestimated. Definitions help us clear away misconceptions about the key issues: Are we sure the antireincarnationist really *understands* the theory he or she is refuting? Likewise, when we try to reconcile reincarnation with Christianity, do we truly understand Christianity *as our Christian challengers define it?* Unless we can establish some common basis of understanding, the reincarnationist and the Christian who is antireincarnation may each be arguing in a language incomprehensible to the other. A discussion, then, of some definitions follows.

Reincarnation Defined

We have, on the surface, the obvious definition of reincarnation: the rebirth of the soul into another body. It's important to separate reincarnation, which teaches rebirth into human form only, from the broader theory of transmigration, which includes soul rebirth into animal (and, in some cases, plant and mineral) form. But beyond this most rudimentary of definitions, there are certain implications that comprise the real issue at hand. We need to share an understanding not only of what reincarnation is, but also of how it works.

First, then, I'd like to reduce reincarnation to three basic premises. These premises can be presented as the heart of reincarnation theory. Then, once we have established the core *theoretical* framework of reincarnation, we can evaluate that theory's impact on one's belief system. The theory and the impact together will make up a clarified definition of what it means to be a "reincarnationist." It is that understanding of reincarnation that we will later go on to reconcile with Christianity.

I can distinctly remember my first exposure to reincarnation. It was in a seventh grade social studies class, and a teacher who was otherwise very knowledgeable told us, when we began studying some of the Eastern cultures, that reincarnation involved the belief that if you were bad you came back as a cow! It was a surprise to me when several years later I encountered Gina

Cerminara's *The World Within* and saw a different view indeed of what reincarnation is all about. How many of our well-intentioned critics hold similar misconceptions?

While all misunderstandings of reincarnation may not be as gross as the example just cited, the prevalence of misconceptions among those who seek to refute the theory convinces me of the value in isolating certain basic premises. For those readers who are familiar with reincarnation, these premises represent nothing new or earth-shaking. Some may even choose to skip ahead to the discussion that comes *after* we have laid this foundation. But for those readers who have had occasion to discuss their beliefs with concerned friends or relatives, the following is offered as a starting place for any step-by-step defense of the reincarnation philosophy. For those readers whose conviction may be antireincarnation, I can only urge that each one lay aside current notions about what reincarnation is and consider the theory in the light of the definitions to follow.

Basic Premises of Reincarnation Philosophy

At its core, I think we can see reincarnation in the following terms:

Life Is Eternal. The first premise of reincarnation theory states that life is eternal. The soul existed before birth just as surely as it will live on after death. In fact, the soul has existence *outside* of time and space. We are ultimately spiritual beings who pass in and out of this three-dimensional planet, with its construct called "time."

This may seem too obvious to bother mentioning, but actually this premise says a lot more than may at first appear. Consider the hundreds of Christian denominations. One of the doctrinal issues that often separates these branches from one another has to do with their different perspectives on eternal life: Does everybody get it or do only some of us get it? Do we attain eternal life through a set of beliefs, affirming a particular faith, or is it how we live our lives that counts? From the various denominations, we get varying shades of difference in the way these questions are answered. But interestingly enough, despite any doctrinal differences, most of these denominations share an underlying assumption that "eternal" means a stretching forever into the future, that you live forever after you die. Yet, by dictionary definition, eternity has no beginning. To be eternal is to be outside of time.

If eternity has no end, neither can it have a beginning. If a life is said to be eternal, then, we must see it as having *neither* beginning nor ending. It is noteworthy that this most basic of reincarnation premises, that life is eternal, adequately deals with the true meaning of eternity.

Life Is Purposeful. The second premise of the reincarnation theory tells us that life is purposeful. For many reincarnationists, this is one of the most appealing aspects of rebirth. In affirming that life is purposeful, reincarnation puts meaning into the most difficult riddles of life. It suggests that there is a real reason for our being here. That purpose, as stated in the Edgar Cayce readings, is to become reconciled with—and even to grow into our full stature as cocreators with—our Father God. The multitudinous experiences of our lifetimes in the earth come to give us the opportunity to learn and grow, to develop our full potential as sons and daughters of God.

Christianity also teaches that there is a purpose in life, and reconciliation with God the Father seems to be central to that purpose. On the surface, the reincarnationist idea of becoming "cocreators" with God presents a point of difference with traditional Christianity, as does the assumption that we are capable of "growing to our full potential"; but even these differences may be more semantic than anything else, as we shall see later.

Life Is Lawful. The third premise underlying the reincarnation philosophy suggests that life is lawful—or that it proceeds according to an orderly set of principles. We are not thrown onto this planet to find out by trial and error how life is supposed to work. There is a set of laws governing this universe, laws that we can learn about and that we can learn to cooperate with. To draw an analogy from physical law, most of us learn everything we need to know about the law of gravity very early in life. Long before we could ever recognize it as a "law" or call it by name, we have watched objects drop and have learned to avoid gravity's unpleasant effects by trying not to fall down. Similarly, we can learn about the laws governing us spiritually through the experiences and observations that our lifetimes in the earth bring to us. The orderliness of life, in fact, becomes the main dynamic around which the reincarnation viewpoint turns, for it teaches us what is creative and what is destructive; what is God-entered and what is self-centered; what is motivated by love and what is motivated by lesser drives. In short, it teaches us how to become all that we can be.

The Reincarnationist Worldview

Life is eternal, purposeful, and orderly. Upon this undergirding we can build our concept of what it means to be a reincarnationist. Yet theoretical definitions are only half of the picture. In order to translate these three basic principles into a belief system, we need to understand them in operational terms; that is, we need to ask ourselves, "How do these premises translate into an approach to life?" As we answer this question, we can see a profile of the reincarnationist's worldview emerging. I would like to examine this worldview closely, for it will be the actual belief system most often criticized by Christians.

Our Identity Is Eternal. Eternal life in the abstract is one thing. The idea that we, as specific identities, may live forever is quite another. But it's important to realize that we all may have different understandings of what it means for our identities to be eternal. How much of this identity we call personality is going to live on, for example? Does reincarnation promise that John Smith, as he is known to himself and the world, will live on? Well, the answer to that question is probably wrapped up in how much John Smith is in touch with his soul or spiritual core. For reincarnation only promises that the core of who we are *spiritually* lives forever. So, in some cases in which a person is truly out of touch with that inner core identity, it may be accurate for that person to say there is no reincarnation! For whenever our sense of who we are is divorced from the spiritual core that *does* live on, the person we *think* we are may not experience survival. Still, that "spiritual core" is not a static, impersonal being, but a living, changing soul, very much involved with the experiences we go through day by day.

In terms of our daily life situations and relationships, our eternal identities ensure each one of us that the person we are today reflects all of the people we have ever been. We have made ourselves what we are and we will continue in that process: The person each one of us is today is a major determinant of what we will be in future experiences. Because we are eternal, shaping ourselves through successive experiences in the earth, each one of us is the master of his or her own destiny. This concept leads us to another very important part of the reincarnationist's belief system:

Free Will Is Supreme. It's amazing how many people think, when they first encounter reincarnation, that it denies free will, that it teaches we are fated by things that happened in the past. Or, worse yet, that when we speak of past lives, we speak of being haunted by the spirits of "other people" who lived in the past. At the very least, under this misguided view, we are powerless to change a fixed destiny that awaits us in this life.

We often see this misconception in Hollywood movies with a reincarnation theme. Peter Proud, attacked by his wife, drowns—just as he did in the prior life. Audrey Rose dies all over again when the memory of her death last time around is awakened. Events from the past loom menacingly on the horizon, binding us in an endless cycle of ill-fated circumstances and premature deaths, these movies seem to say.

But actually, reincarnation suggests that the *choices* we make every moment of our lives determine our destiny. No one is "fated" to a particular life course, be it gloomy or sunny. We are free to choose at every moment.

Now, of course, even the most unrestrained will cannot make major life changes instantaneously. Choices work in complex chains, building on one another. Most of us could not totally change our lives as of tomorrow just by deciding to today. We would have to begin by making certain choices that would *eventually* alter our lives, just as our past choices have gradually built the circumstances we are in today. For example, suppose you had chosen in the past to attend a social gathering, and there you met someone who sparked your interest in a particular career path. That interest, in turn, made you choose a certain school for training. While at that school, you met the person you eventually married. Whatever the chain of choices may have been, it would be unrealistic to expect to undo a whole chain of choices in a flash.

So our lives are predetermined by past incarnations *only to the extent that we choose to perpetuate certain choices.* Our freedom is preserved in the fact that we can begin to make a new chain of choices, leading us in a whole new direction, at any moment. Indeed, learning to make appropriate use of that tremendous freedom is at the heart of what life is all about, according to the reincarnation philosophy.

Life Is an Opportunity. This belief follows closely from the affirmation that we are here on earth in order to use our free wills wisely. Ironically, reincarnation can often appear to be a philosophy that denies the good of the body and the value of life on earth. The person of Christian belief will say, "God created us to live on this earth. My Bible teaches me that my body will even resurrect. Yet reincarnation teaches that the body is something to be escaped."

While it is true that some reincarnationist schools of thought see the body as a shackle from which we seek freedom, this is not the approach of the Edgar Cayce readings. There are few sources that speak more enthusiastically about life in the physical body and the supreme opportunity of life in the earth. These readings suggest that the human body is God's very special gift to us, and that its potential is nothing short of expressing the spirit in the earth. In approaching bodily life with an attitude of hope and even joy, we fulfill our spiritual potential as well, these readings tell us, for our God means for us to be happy. This point brings us to the last—and perhaps most important—aspect of the reincarnationist's belief system.

We Are Loved by a Merciful God, but Still We Must Learn. Theists of all persuasions must deal with a very disturbing paradox: How can God be all-loving and all-powerful at the same time? A quick look around us reveals many conditions which naggingly suggest that God cannot be both all-loving and all-powerful. Why do the innocent suffer? Why do the selfish and even ruthless often seem to prosper? Many an agnostic is lost to religion on the grounds that he or she cannot love a God so merciless as to allow human suffering, when it is in His power to end it, nor respect a God who is powerless to end human suffering, despite His wish to do so.

I would not presume to resolve the philosophical problem of evil. This problem has baffled philosophers and theologians throughout history, and whatever comments could be made here would add little to the volumes that have already been written on the subject. The most I can hope to do is present the perspective that reincarnation lends to this age-old paradox.

As presented in the Cayce readings, the God of the reincarnationist is merciful. Further, the God of the Cayce reincarnation readings is a loving parent—not one who is uninterested, removed, or impersonal. He is not standing there, waiting to condemn us, but is instead ready to forgive and to allow us to make a fresh start whenever we ask Him for mercy.

But, at the same time—and here's the condition that we sometimes rail against—our God also insists that we learn from life's experiences. This means that sometimes we must be allowed to experience the unpleasant consequences of the choices we have made. Sometimes the consequences come quickly, within the span of one lifetime; other times they are delayed. But just as the good parents will not continually bail their child out every time the youngster gets in trouble, God knows that our "adulthood" as souls depends in part on how well we mature through learning from our mistakes.

It should not be taken from this that every unpleasant circumstance in life comes as punishment for some misdeed. In the complexity of the soul's life experiences, some are chosen for the inner fortitude they will help develop, as in the taking on of a physical handicap, for example. Others may be chosen for the service they will provide to others. The Cayce readings cite Down's syndrome children as a notable example of this, suggesting that the souls entering this particular experience provide an opportunity for those around them to learn a very special kind of love.

But even when life's adversities do come as the consequences of poor choices in the past, the Cayce readings concur with the Bible in saying that God allows us no more than what we are able to bear. While it seems that many people are faced with unbearable circumstances in life, we might understand this to be an assurance that, no matter how catastrophic an experience may be, there is full awareness of God's support and unconditional love on the soul level.

The reincarnationist and even the most fundamental of Christians, then, share belief in a God who both loves us and holds us accountable for our actions. Of course, we must deal with the question of whether there are material differences in the fundamental Christian's and the reincarnationist's understanding of *how* that love is expressed and *how* that accountability is required, but such issues will be better dealt with in chapter 14. In the meantime, we can summarize the reincarnationist belief system in this way:

We are eternal, spiritual beings whose primary purpose in life is reconciliation with our Creator. Through the opportunity of human experiences in the earth, and because of the mercy of our loving God, we are able to use our free will to learn and grow. The earth is the school where we can learn the consequences of our choices, both constructive and destructive. If we learn to make constructive choices over destructive ones, we mature spiritually and grow toward being the companions to Himself that God has always intended us to be.

Christian Faith Is Not Inherent Within Reincarnation

I want first to point out that there is nothing inherently Christian (or non-Christian, for that matter) in the reincarnationist philosophy I have outlined here. I make no claim that reincarnation is a Christian belief, any more than I would claim that Republicanism is a Christian political party. That is, while the most casual observation will tell us that not all Republicans are Christians, many Christians (even Democratic Christians!) would allow that it's entirely possible to be a Republican and a Christian at the same time. The point is, that while nothing in the Republican platform *requires* Christian belief, the fundamental Christian would find no conflict in being a Republican—just as long as nothing in the Republican platform violated his or her basic Christian beliefs.

This analogy to political party obviously breaks down if carried too far. Reincarnation has a lot more to do with souls and redemption than Republicanism does, and so its potential for violating basic Christian beliefs is higher. As we continue this discussion, we will be examining whether there is such a violation. My aim in raising the point at this juncture is simply to emphasize that reincarnation cannot fairly be denounced by fundamental Christians simply because it fails to be Christian in itself. It must be kept in mind that the issue at stake here is not whether reincarnation *always* implies Christian faith, but whether there is a legitimate place for fundamental Christians among the broader population of reincarnationists.

But before we can go on to address adequately that issue, it's important that we make sure we know just what we will be reconciling reincarnation *with*. We must define the Christian beliefs which we hope to reconcile with reincarnation.

Basic Christian Issues Defined

In the introduction I drew a distinction between "Christianity" as a general term and those branches of Christianity that alternately call themselves "fundamental," "Evangelical," or "biblical" Christianity. In the context of this distinction, then, I would like to identify the three fundamental Christian beliefs that must be at the core of any attempted reconciliation with reincarnation. Unless we can present reincarnation as compatible with these pillars of Christian faith, the theory indeed has no place in the more doctrinally conservative Christian's personal beliefs.

We Are Saved Through Faith in Jesus. This belief is the cornerstone of the more fundamental Christian understanding concerning the role of Jesus in our salvation. It's not enough to describe Jesus as a good man and a good example. From the perspective of this more fundamental or Evangelical Christian, one cannot claim to be a Christian without first coming to the point of saying, "I can't make it on my own. I believe that Jesus has done it for me, and I accept the gift of salvation that He has to offer."

Through the life, death, and resurrection of Jesus Christ, the only perfect Son of God, salvation was made possible. Through His death, an atonement was made for our sins, and only through believing in and accepting that atonement can we look forward to eternal peace with Him in heaven. The heart of Evangelical Christianity, then, is in the saving faith which reconciles us to the Father and establishes the salvation of our souls.

The person with this kind of Christian faith is likely to see reincarnation as a philosophy which teaches that we save ourselves through learning how to become good people; *we* make *ourselves* perfect; we work our way to heaven. For one whose Bible clearly teaches that we don't work our way to heaven but get there through faith in Jesus, this belief is unacceptable. Unless we can deal adequately with this objection, our reconciliation attempt is most certainly a lost cause! For salvation through Jesus is the true *biblical* basis of Christian faith, these Christians believe; and there is no higher authority than Scripture.

The Bible Is the Ultimate Authority on Doctrinal Matters. Evangelical or fundamental Christianity is essentially "biblical Christianity," in the sense that all of its doctrines are believed to be taken directly from what the Bible teaches. Therefore, a doctrine such as reincarnation must be evaluated in the light of Scripture, if such a Christian is to determine its compatibility with his or her faith.

There is a further consideration to be dealt with in reasoning with those who hold to the Bible as the ultimate authority on doctrinal matters. It is only reasonable for a Bible-believing Christian to ask, "If reincarnation is true, why didn't the Bible mention it? I just can't believe that the Bible would leave out something that important." Unless we can answer *this* question satisfactorily, we cannot hope to make a case for reincarnation's being compatible with biblical Christianity.

There is one more basic Christian doctrine that should be identified as essential to our discussion of reincarnation and fundamental Christian faith.

Those Who Are "Saved" Will One Day Be Given Resurrected Bodies. This is a very important aspect of the biblically based Christian concept of salvation. The salvation and eternal life promised in the Bible are not seen as merely a spiritual afterlife but as an existence in a perfect, resurrected body. This body will be like the earthly one the believer has known, according to this doctrine, only it will be perfect—without weakness, sickness, or death.

To those who hold such a belief, reincarnation seems to be a direct contradiction to the promise of a resurrected body. After all, if we have experienced hundreds or even thousands of lives, in hundreds and even thousands of bodies, which one will be the resurrected body? A question more basic still is whether there is even a place for a resurrected body in the reincarnationist belief system. Doesn't reincarnation teach that the body is like a shell to be discarded at the end of an earthly sojourn, these Christians might ask?

Once again, we would have to answer that not *all* reincarnationists expect to spend their hereafter in a resurrected body. But for those reincarnationists who also happen to be Christians, there is truly a place for the resurrected body in the ultimate destiny of the human being. There is also an explanation of how this resurrected body fits in among the multitudinous incarnations the soul may have experienced, but that explanation will have to wait until other, more central, Christian objections to reincarnation have been addressed.

Now my reincarnationist readers should not get caught up on the question of whether *they personally* accept the three basic criteria identified above. Regardless of whether one does or does not accept the saving role of Jesus, the ultimate authority of Scripture, and the doctrine of the bodily resurrection, it is still important that we agree on these criteria as the "ground rules" of our subsequent discussion. For unless we can show reincarnation to be *potentially* compatible with these doctrines, we have no hope of reconciling this philosophy with the more doctrinally conservative versions of Christianity. The reincarnationist need not embrace these beliefs in order to respect them as necessary to any reconciliation with such Christian faith. Just as I previously urged the antireincarnationist not to reject reincarnation simply because it was not inherently Christian, I now urge the more doctrinally liberal reincarnationist not to throw out the more conservative criteria as invalid. The point of this reconciliation is not to make all reincarnationists into biblically centered, doctrinally conservative Christians any more than it is to turn all Christians into reincarnationists. The point is rather to see if the two views are compatible enough to *allow* belief in both at the same time.

Now, having defined some of the key issues for both the reincarnationist and the person of conservative Christian faith and having used these definitions to establish a common understanding, we can go on to look at the next steps to reconciling these two points of view.

13

Removing the Obstacles to Integration

THIS IS CERTAINLY not the first attempt to reconcile reincarnation with Christianity. How many lectures have been given with this aim in mind? How many pamphlets and books written? How many people have entered the debate with friends and family members? Why, then, another attempt? For me, the reason is this simple: I have not yet encountered anything in print that attempts reconciliation on the basis of those core or fundamental Christian doctrines discussed above.

Sometimes, in not understanding the beliefs of Christians who hold to those core doctrines as the essence of Christianity (or at least in not being willing to accept their ground rules), well-meaning reincarnationists have created more barriers than they tear down. In presenting proreincarnation arguments that are not consistent with the ground rules we have established here, the reincarnationist can inadvertently strengthen the notion that the reincarnationist and the Christian whose faith rests on these core doctrines have nothing in common. The next essential step, then, is to identify those human-made obstacles and point out why they are counterproductive to any reconciliation of reincarnation with Christianity.

The "By the Fruits You Shall Know Them" Argument

The most reasonable argument in the world, to many reincarnationists, proceeds along these lines: Jesus Himself told us we should judge by the fruits. As I look around and see people who have come to embrace a belief in reincarnation, I see people who are taking responsibility for their own lives; I see people who are growing, overcoming their bad traits, and improving their relationships with other people. In short, I see good fruits all around me. Therefore, by Jesus' own criterion, "By the fruits you shall know them," we have clear evidence that belief in reincarnation is good.

The problem with this seemingly airtight argument is that the antireincarnationist Christian is looking at an entirely different type of "fruit" than what the reincarnationist is pointing to. If, as some Christians believe, belief in reincarnation makes it impossible for a person to accept Jesus as Savior, then the ultimate "fruit" of reincarnation belief is the loss of that person's soul. All the temporal, short-term "good fruits" in the world can't possibly make up for such a devastating ultimate "fruit."

We can see an analogy in one literal fruit, the apple. People would probably agree that, in general, the apple is a healthful food, a good fruit. But hidden within the apple are seeds that contain deadly cyanide. Taken in great enough quantity, those apple seeds could kill a person. This good fruit, then, also has the potential to be a bad fruit, depending on how it is consumed. Likewise, if the doctrine of reincarnation has hidden within it something that is antithetical to Christian faith, then for the Christian who believes this, reincarnation thinking's potential danger is death (or eternal damnation) to the soul. That's about as bad a "fruit" as we can imagine!

Until we have shown that reincarnation need not exclude faith in Jesus, we cannot be surprised when some of our Christian friends are unimpressed with the "fruits" argument. They are not denying Jesus' criterion. In fact, they are even using it to build the case *against* reincarnation.

Arguing on the Basis of Church History

It is very common for defenders of reincarnation to claim that the teaching of rebirth originally *was* in the Bible, but that it was edited out due to church politics. Whether such allegations are true is beside the point, and so I will not devote space here to recapping the details of these charges. The crucial point is this: The person of biblically centered faith has already set the Bible as the source of all doctrine. Any argument that attempts to undermine the Bible's veracity thus destroys all basis of further discussion with that person. That Christian is saying, "The Bible in front of me is true, was inspired by God, and tells me everything I need to know in matters of spiritual import." The reincarnationist responds by saying, "Well, there are big gaps in the Bible. Somebody cut it up years ago." Regardless of whether such a claim is true, for that Christian there is no longer any basis for discussion.

There is still another pitfall in arguing on the basis of church history. Many reincarnationists will cite the beliefs of certain Church Fathers as evidence that reincarnation was once a part of Christian theology. One problem with that approach is that those few Church Fathers who did espouse something like reincarnation were not expressing the majority opinion of their day. It seems the most we can say is that reincarnation thinking among some Christians is nothing new. As long ago as the first century, it was prevalent enough to be a point of redhot debate.

We must also keep returning to the central importance of the Bible as the basis of biblically centered Christian doctrine. For biblical Christianity prides itself on drawing its beliefs not from the ever-changing opinions of theologians, but from the steadfast foundation of Scripture itself. So even if we could prove conclusively that a portion of the early Church Fathers were confirmed reincarnationists, that would not in itself win the case for reincarnation. Only if we could show scriptural evidence for their position could we hope to use the Church Fathers as an argument. Yet, ironically, it is in the well-intentioned attempt to defend reincarnation on the basis of Scripture that the reincarnationist often makes the gravest mistake.

Arguing by "Proof Texting" Supposed Reincarnation Passages

How often have we seen defenses that use passages from the Bible to support the concept of reincarnation and to build a case for the theory indeed being taught there if only we would look for it? Such an approach is called "proof texting," and the problem with it is that a *proof* text usually ignores a *con*text! Probably all of us have had at one time or another the frustration of seeing a Bible verse taken out of context in order to prove us wrong on some debated point of doctrine. Unfortunately, reincarnationists can do the same thing when it comes to defending their beliefs. They proof text whenever they take isolated passages out of the Bible and use them in support of reincarnation. But the uncomfortable fact is that most of the supposed reincarnation passages fall apart under scrutiny, doing the reincarnationist position far more harm than good.

Therefore, I'm going to ask my reincarnationist readers to engage with me in tearing down some cherished notions of how the Bible deals with reincarnation. This is not such a destructive move as it might seem: By removing what I plan to show is a false foundation for reconciliation, we make way for a new foundation that can better stand the scrutiny of close Bible study.

A Refutation of Some Apparent Reincarnation Passages in the Bible

- John 3:7—"Ye must be born again." If that doesn't sound like reincarnation, I don't know what does. But if we read the whole chapter, we'll see that Jesus goes into a very careful discussion of how birth in the flesh and birth in the spirit are two totally different things. This is made especially clear when Nicodemus asks Jesus how it is possible to be born again. He questions the possibility of returning to one's mother's womb. At this point Jesus most definitely makes a distinction between rebirth physically and rebirth spiritually. In this context, we can only conclude that when Jesus says, "Ye must be born again," He is talking about a spiritual rebirth. Only blind determination to see reincarnation in the Bible could twist this passage into a reincarnation verse.

- Matthew 17:12 and 13—"But I say unto you, That Elias is come already, and they knew him not, but have done unto him whatsoever they listed. Likewise shall also the Son of man suffer of them. Then the disciples understood that he spake unto them of John the Baptist." How can we get around the fact that Jesus Himself identified John the Baptist as the return of Elias? At first, this looks like the perfect reincarnation proof text. Yet closer examination suggests that we should be cautious in citing this episode as proof of reincarnation in the Bible.

For one thing, there was a popularly held belief among the Jews of Jesus' day that certain of the prophets would return. This was not at all the same as reincarnation. The prophets were not expected to return as part of the reincarnation cycle of birth, death, and rebirth, but rather in a special dispensation—a sort of cameo appearance, if you will! Note, for example, the guesses people made concerning Jesus' own identity: "Some say that thou art John the Baptist: some, Elias; and others, Jeremias, or one of the prophets." (Matthew 16:14) How could the people have considered Jesus to be the reappearance of John the Baptist—Jesus' own contemporary—who had been so recently executed? Clearly their speculations are predicated upon something other than reincarnation as we understand it.

We can add the fact that the Gospel of Luke describes John the Baptist as coming "in the spirit and power of Elias" (Luke 1:17), indicating that John filled an Elias-like role. All of this considered, we are on shaky ground when we hold up Jesus' testimony that John the Baptist was Elias as evidence of reincarnation in the Bible.

- Galatians 6:7—" . . . whatsoever a man soweth, that shall he also reap." There is no doubt that this concept is *compatible* with reincarnation. But does it *teach* it? At first, we may say "yes," because as we look around us we can see lots of people not sowing what they reap within the framework of a single lifetime. Therefore, the logic goes, we must take reincarnation into consideration in order to see Galatians 6:7 as a true statement.

This line of reasoning carries pitfalls similar to those in the "fruits" argument discussed earlier. Because again, from the perspective of traditional Christian thinking, the fate of the soul after death is a crucial part of the picture. It's true that people *appear* not to reap what they sow, but they *will* do so in the hereafter. It is a mistake, then, to hold this passage up as one that only makes sense in the light of reincarnation.

• John 9:2—"Master, who did sin, this man, or his parents, that he was born blind?" Perhaps this is the closest we come to a true reincarnation passage in the Bible. It is a special favorite of mine because, while I cannot make it "prove" reincarnation, I can see it as rich with implications.

Jesus and His disciples encounter the man born blind, and for some reason the disciples are prompted to ask their Master whose sin (his or his parents') was responsible for the man's unfortunate situation. From their question, we can infer that Jesus' disciples at least entertained the idea that the man could have sinned before he was born. Their question strongly implied at least some *speculation* concerning an existence prior to physical birth, in which we are responsible for our actions. It is not too far-fetched to assert on the basis of this account that Jesus' disciples were at the very least curious about reincarnation. It is even understandable if some readers go so far as to infer that some of the disciples may have held reincarnation as part of their own belief systems.

Be that as it may, we can focus on the fact that Jesus' own disciples asked that extraordinary question and may miss the truly illuminating aspect of this story. For in Jesus' *response* to them, we may get a glimpse of the Master's own views regarding reincarnation. More than that, in the way Jesus handles this situation, we may have the key to understanding how reincarnation fits in with what His ministry was all about.

Jesus and the Man Born Blind: Key to Jesus' Views on Reincarnation. The response Jesus gave to the question about the man born blind was one which had the effect of refocusing His questioners. In essence He said, "Wait a minute. There's a third possibility that you haven't even considered: 'Neither hath this man sinned, nor his parents: but that the works of God should be made manifest in him.'" (John 9:3) Here Jesus seems to be guiding His disciples away from a mechanistic view which automatically assigns guilt or blame for every undesirable circumstance. He is asking them to turn from a focus on cut-and-dried, cause-and-effect thinking (or karma), as typified by the codified law of His day, and look instead at the action of grace in the human life. The answer Jesus gives His disciples clearly indicates that the man's condition should be seen as an opportunity for Him to show the power and the love of God. He goes on to heal the man, and we can be sure that many lives were touched in a deep and lasting way as a result of witnessing that miracle.

Now what observations can we draw from this account? Thinking back to our earlier discussion of the basic premises and beliefs involved in reincarnation philosophy, we can ask whether the blind man had deliberately chosen his lot in life in order to be the occasion for others to experience the reality of God, or whether this was a case of Jesus' turning a man's punishment into a beautiful demonstration of love and forgiveness. It is not for us to know the answer to that question, but either way the message is the same: Jesus' work involved a better way for the human soul, a way of compassion and forgiveness instead of a legalistic "measuring up."

The Lord used this same refocusing tactic to express important truths in other situations as well. For example, when the adulteress is brought before Him, Jesus is presented with a double-bind situation. If He condemns the woman, He violates all of His own teachings of love and forgiveness. On the other hand, if He tells her captors to let her go free, He contradicts the law that He claims to be fulfilling. "He that is without sin among you, let him first cast a stone" shifts the focus once again from such legalistic thinking to Jesus' own emphasis on forgiveness. (John 8:7)

Consider, too, the circumstances under which Jesus chooses to reveal His own identity as the Christ. In response to the disciples' reports that people are speculating that Jesus is John the Baptist or one of the prophets, He asks, "But whom say ye that I am?" (Matthew 16:15) It is here that Peter steps forward and affirms Jesus' Christhood: "Thou art the Christ, the Son of the living God." (verse 16)

Notice what has happened. Once again Jesus has refocused relatively fruitless speculation in order to reveal an important truth. In this case, He has used it to bring about Peter's awakening to the true nature of his Master's person and work. Jesus is the Christ, the Promised One, the Savior! Appropriately enough, this becomes the historic occasion upon which Jesus voices the central truth of His church. For it is here that Simon is actually given his name, Peter (literally, "rock"), and Jesus states that

" ... upon this rock I will build my church ... " (verse 18) Was Jesus building His church on Peter, the *person,* or on the immense significance of Peter's *realization?* Obviously something important happened when Peter recognized Jesus' Christhood. It was as though for the first time he grasped the full impact of his Master's identity and mission.

We, too, must come to grips with Jesus' mission when we ask why, if reincarnation is true, did He not overtly teach such an important concept? Actually, when we examine Jesus' role as Messiah, we may see that He had good reason to avoid teaching the concept of reincarnation. As the promised Messiah, He had come to usher in a new order in the relationship between God and man and to show that He was offering the law of grace as an alternative to the legalistic (or karmic, if you will) approach. Everything in Jesus' ministry bespoke fulfillment of the law—not through following rules and regulations, but through *being* all that the law was designed to help man to be.

Jesus came not to be just one more in a long line of teachers of the law; He came to be the fulfillment of it. It was, therefore, essential that He shift attention, wherever possible, *away* from questions like "Who sinned, this man or his parents, that he was born blind?" and *toward* the perfect truth that His whole life demonstrated: that in fulfilling the law, He was reconciling God and man in a way never before possible. How it would have watered down Jesus' message of freedom from the law for Him to have spent His days teaching reincarnation, with all of its focus on cause and effect! In fact, I submit that for Jesus to have made a formal teaching of reincarnation would have been tantamount to His merely reiterating Old Testament law. His mission was highly focused. He came as Messiah, not just another spiritual expositor!

The important item, then, is not whether we can find a record in the Bible of Jesus ever teaching reincarnation. The real issue, if we're going to reconcile reincarnation with Christianity, is whether the beliefs involved in reincarnation are consistent with the ministry of a Messiah who came to show the way of grace. In the next chapter I plan to show that the answer is clearly "yes."

14

A Plan for Integration

IN THE PRECEDING chapter, we considered the possibility that Jesus was deliberately silent on the subject of reincarnation. If this is true, then it would not be a surprise to find the New Testament as a whole equally silent on the subject. We could easily see that this silence would spring directly from Jesus' own strategy of moving His listeners' attention from karma to grace. It would be redundant for the New Covenant (as we may also call the New Testament) to reiterate the concept of responsibility under the law that is so characteristic of reincarnation. Instead, we would expect to find an emphasis on the work of a Messiah who came to usher in the way of grace for the human soul.

Silence concerning reincarnation, then, would not be evidence against its compatibility with Christianity. A direct denunciation of it—or even a passing comment of denial—would, however, preclude the biblically based Christian's acceptance of reincarnation. It is very important to keep in mind that Scripture is that Christian's ultimate authority on doctrinal matters. For anyone recognizing the authority of the Bible as absolute, nothing would be more incompatible with the ministry of Jesus than a teaching that is denounced or denied by Scripture.

Therefore, before we develop any systematic arguments for the compatibility of reincarnation with the work of Jesus, we must satisfy the basic requirement that belief in reincarnation is not forbidden by Scripture.

Does the Bible Teach Against Reincarnation?

Does the Bible ever say that there is no reincarnation? It's one thing to point out alternate interpretations for supposed *pro*reincarnation passages, as we did in the last chapter. But what about *anti*reincarnation passages? Are there any? Does the Bible anywhere condemn the idea of reincarnation or take a stand that is so clearly counter to it that reincarnation is just not a tenable position for the fundamental Christian to hold? While an exhaustive survey of Scripture is beyond the scope of this work, there are some key passages that we should examine in order to answer these questions adequately.

Another Look at the Man Born Blind. Let's return first to the passage we considered at some length in the last chapter—the story of Jesus and the man born blind. In our initial consideration of this story, we focused on the fact that Jesus did not use His disciples' extraordinary question, "Who sinned, this man or his parents, that he was born blind?" as an opportunity to affirm the truth of reincarnation. But there is something else Jesus did not do on that occasion: He did not use that question as an opportunity to *deny* reincarnation!

Consider the full implication of this omission on Jesus' part. This question came from among His own disciples. It was not an idle question posed by a passerby, nor was it the kind of "trick" question those in authority sometimes asked in attempts to entrap Him. It was instead a genuine question from the very people He was preparing to carry the Gospel once He left this earth. These same men, as Jesus no doubt knew, would be instrumental in the writing of what was to become the New Testament. Yet when they ask, "Who sinned, this man or his parents, that he was born blind?" Jesus *does not* seize the opportunity to nip such a terrible heresy in the bud. He does not say, "How could you consider the possibility that the man sinned before he was born?" He lets a golden opportunity to deny or warn against reincarnation go by. We can only ask ourselves why Jesus let this opportunity go by, if reincarnation is indeed such a false and dangerous belief.

Jesus' own failure to denounce reincarnation is perhaps the strongest case we can make for the absence of antireincarnation teaching in the Bible. But before we can safely assert that the rest of the Bible does indeed follow Jesus' lead and remain silent with respect to reincarnation, we must face the one verse most often used as the definitive antireincarnation Bible text: " . . . it is appointed unto men once to die, but after this the judgment . . . " (Hebrews 9:27)

A Discussion of Hebrews 9:27. On the surface this verse might be taken as a categorical statement that we die only once and then face the judgment day. If we die only once, then it follows that we live only once. How can such a statement be anything other than a direct contradiction of reincarnation? Once again, the answer comes with careful examination of the contextual framework from which this passage is lifted. We will find that when we take the time to examine context, this passage goes the way of most proof texts.

Just as we saw our favorite proreincarnation verses melt before the scrutiny of contextual consideration, so does this antireincarnation verse lose its punch when we look at the entire chapter in which it appears. Indeed, this verse, as it is so often quoted by antireincarnationists, isn't even a complete sentence! The complete sentence reads:

"And as it is appointed unto men once to die, but after this the judgment: So Christ was once offered to bear the sins of many; and unto them that look for Him shall he appear the second time without sin unto salvation."

The complete sentence places quite a different interpretation on the oft-quoted fragment in Hebrews 9:27, for it seems to be making a statement not about reincarnation but about the work of Christ. In order to appreciate fully the import of the beautiful truth expressed in Hebrews 9:28 and 29, we should look at the discussion that leads up to it. For these verses are the conclusion of a most significant chapter. As such, they are best understood in the light of the discourse for which they are the culmination.

There is little point in repeating an entire chapter of Scripture here. Instead, I would encourage my readers to go to their own Bibles and read the entire ninth chapter of the book of Hebrews. For in it we have not only a more illuminating understanding of those final verses quoted above, but also a statement concerning the central issue in the reincarnation and Christianity controversy: the atoning work of Christ.

In surveying the ninth chapter of Hebrews, we see that it discusses how Christ's sacrifice on the cross was both a continuation of, and a great contrast to, the sacrificial system of the Old Testament. Repeatedly, this chapter stresses that the temple sacrifices made in the past were needed yearly because they were imperfect, incomplete. Throughout the chapter, we have a contrast drawn between the yearly sacrifice made in the temple and the once and for all, finished work of Christ. This point builds to a culmination beginning in the 25th verse, where it says:

> Nor yet that he should offer himself often, as the high priest entereth into the holy place every year with blood of others; For then must he often have suffered since the foundation of the world: but now once in the end of the world hath he appeared to put away sin by the sacrifice of himself. And as it is appointed unto men once to die, but after this the judgment: So Christ was once offered to bear the sins of many; and unto them that look for him shall he appear the second time without sin unto salvation. Hebrews 9:25-28

The context, then, is a comprehensive treatment of how the work of Christ forever changed the order of things between God and man.

Keeping this broad context in mind, let's go on to a closer examination of that crucial word "once," so frequently used in the ninth chapter of Hebrews. In verses 26-28, it is used three times: *"once* in the end of the world," *"once* to die, but after this the judgment," and "So Christ was *once* offered to bear the sins . . . " Can we conclude that all of these "onces" mean "one single time," or can we see "once" also in the connotation of "once upon a time"? Within the book of Hebrews, we have evidence that the word is used in both connotations.

For example, we read of the high priest going "once

every year" to make his sacrifices (9:7), and we see Christ "once offered to bear the sins." (9:28) But we also have reference to those who were "once enlightened," but now have fallen away (6:4) and to those who "once purged" should have no more conscience of sin. (10:2) To confuse the issue even more, verse 26 tells us that Christ appeared once in the end of the world, but verse 28 tells us that He will appear a second time to those who look for Him. In all of these verses, "once" is translated from the same Greek word (hapax). Yet there is a clear difference in nuance, the word implying sometimes a single event, sometimes more generally an event from the past.

It seems clear that Christ's once-and-for-all sacrifice requires an emphasis on the single event connotation of "once." It is the only emphasis that provides proper contrast to the repeated sacrifices that came before. But there is another contrast equally important to the meaning of the ninth chapter of Hebrews: the contrast between the way things once were (using "once" in the more general sense) and the way they are now that Christ has made the perfect sacrifice. In this context, mankind did once die, just as I Corinthians 15:22 tells us that " . . . in Adam all die . . . "

This death in Adam is the only death that would take on meaning against the backdrop of Hebrews 9. Why would the writer digress in the middle of his thematic dissertation concerning the work of Christ to make a statement about how many lives we live? And why, even if that were the intent, did the writer talk about the number of times we die rather than the number of times we live? If it had been the writer's intent to warn us against the "false doctrine" of reincarnation, wouldn't he have made a more direct, less ambiguous comment? It seems much truer to the context to see this passage as a juxtaposition of the perpetual state of death that came in

Adam with the once-and-for-all sacrifice Christ made to free us from this death. Just as I Corinthians 15:22 contrasts death in Adam with being made alive in Christ, our passage in Hebrews contrasts spiritual death and the continual sacrifice it necessitated with the single, momentous event in history which had the power to "put away sin." (verse 26)

Once again we are led back to the central point in the reconciliation of reincarnation with Christianity: Can we harmonize the implications of karma and rebirth with a Christ who "appeared to put away sin by the sacrifice of himself"? The response to this question must be found in a context even larger than that of Hebrews 9.

A Holistic View of the Bible

Most Christian thinkers would be among the first to affirm that the work of Christ came as the culmination of a long process that began in Eden. The coming of the Messiah was not something that suddenly occurred, without foreshadowing and without antecedents. It was instead the climax of a plan that began to unfold almost from the time of our appearance on earth. As we begin to trace the development of that plan and the process of its unfoldment, we also find evidence for the essential compatibility of reincarnation and Christianity. For in seeing how the work of Christ perfected the plan that was laid in Eden, we will also see how it completed the work that karma alone was insufficient to accomplish.

The Pattern Begins in Eden. Almost from the beginning of the first biblical account of mankind's existence, we find the story of a creature who chooses to defy its creator. In traditional Christian terms, we may see in the first chapters of Genesis the story of "the Fall," from which mankind has ever since needed to be rescued or redeemed. Some reincarnationists might see the Fall as a rebellion of cosmic proportions, separating us from the God with whom we must ultimately be reunited; others might see it as a necessary—albeit painful—step in a maturation process that must eventually return us to our Creator as spiritually adult beings. But whatever light we might cast on the events reported in the first three chapters of Genesis, one condition remains constant: In Eden there was the choice of self-will over God's will, and it was that choice which resulted in mankind's being "lost" spiritually. Our question is, can Christianity's prescription for lost souls work within a reincarnationist belief system?

The answer to this question is not a simple one. It cannot be given in a sentence, a paragraph, or any single, conclusive Bible text. Instead, it requires the careful reconstruction of the Christian plan of salvation. We must trace this plan back to its earliest antecedents in order to see how the way of grace, made perfect in Jesus, superseded karma and the law without abolishing it. Volumes have been written about the plan of salvation as it unfolds from Genesis to Revelation. My purpose here is not to make yet another attempt at a theological analysis that has already been done by others far more qualified than I. Rather, I have chosen to point out some highlights that have particular significance for our ability to see the place of reincarnation within the historical context of Christian salvation.

In Genesis 3 we read of two significant events immediately following the disobedience of Adam and Eve. As a consequence of their choosing to defy God, they are driven from the Garden, the cherubim and flaming sword guarding against their return. But even before the banishment of Adam and Eve, God had already begun the plan for their safe return some day. For in the third chapter of Genesis we have what theologians generally agree is the very first Messianic promise: the seed of the woman shall "bruise [the serpent's] head." (Genesis 3:15) Thus begins the thread of an ageless promise that we can follow through the pages of the Old Testament to its perfection in the New. In fact, the banishment and the Messianic promise form twin threads that will ultimately weave Old Testament together with New, law together with grace, reincarnation together with Christianity. But that is not to happen yet in our biblical story. First, we must see each of the threads developed individually.

We next pick up the twin threads at the time of the Flood. This first recorded natural disaster can be identified as a major event in the unfoldment of God's plan for our ultimate reconciliation with Him. In the light of the Cayce readings on earth changes, we understand that our thoughts, our deeds, our innermost lives have a direct and collective effect on our environment—to the extent that the earth itself can respond to our collective thinking. The Flood was a dramatic demonstration for mankind on the earth at that time that the human being is subject to the law of cause and effect, spiritually as well as physically. Doesn't the Bible itself tell us that the Flood came as a direct result of the people's wickedness?

In one sense, then, we may see the Flood as mankind's first lesson in the law of cause and effect. It was a devastating experience in reaping the results of their destructive ways. Just as the act of disobedience in Eden made banishment from the Garden necessary, the later decadence of the people brought the Flood upon them. Thus, we have the thread of law taking on more definition in the experience of mankind. God was making it clear that certain standards of conduct were required and that certain consequences would result from a failure to meet those standards. The concept is identical to that of karma.

Just as the Flood's lesson concerning cause and effect continued the thread begun with the banishment from

Eden, the promise God made to Noah after the Flood continued the thread begun with that first Messianic promise. He promises never again to destroy the earth by flood and calls that promise a covenant with Noah and all of his descendants. This is the first of the covenants between God and us, and in it we find the same thread of promise, mercy, and reconciliation that was indicated when God promised to overcome Satan through the descendants of Eve. It would be well for us to examine this covenant and the others that were to come after it, for they become the central theme as the plan of salvation unfolds.

A Look at Covenant and Law. A covenant is an agreement, a binding contract between two parties. The promise made by God at the end of the Flood is clearly of this nature:

> And I, behold, I establish my covenant with you, and with your seed after you . . . neither shall there any more be a flood to destroy the earth. Genesis 9:9, and 11

From this first recorded covenant we can trace a series of increasingly defined contracts that embody the two threads begun in Eden. One thread will have to do with humankind's responsibility to behave in certain ways, to live according to certain laws or rules of conduct. The other thread will have to do with the unfailing mercy of God, despite humankind's failure to live up to its end of the bargain. We will see in the first thread the basic structure of karmically or law-oriented reconciliation. We will see in the second the development of grace, perfected in the atonement made by Christ. And we will see in the weaving of these two the reconciliation of reincarnation and Christianity.

Perhaps the most well known of all the covenants in the Old Testament is the one in which God promises that He will make of Abram (later Abraham) a great nation (Genesis 15:18) and a blessing to all nations (Genesis 12:3). In the establishment of this promise through the descendants (both physical and spiritual) of Abraham, we can see an emphasis on the development of a promise that will endure through history. The covenants were not temporary provisional agreements, but rather the substance of God's relationship to the human race as long as we live on this earth. The covenant may develop as it is defined and refined over history, but the essential contract between God and humankind remains immutable.

As we see during the time of Moses, the covenant does indeed become increasingly complex, embodying the law under which Israel is to operate. The importance of this law is driven home when we read in Deuteronomy, "Keep therefore the words of this covenant, and do them, that ye may prosper in all that ye do." (Deut. 29:9) Once again we see a clear relationship spelled out between our behavior and the consequences it will bring in life; in other words, cause and effect. From those early lessons concerning cause and effect in Eden and at the time of the Flood, the scriptural account has gone on to develop a definitive articulation of Law, with a capital "L." The law of cause and effect has been codified into specific rules of conduct. The terms of the contract have been clearly spelled out for us.

In the terms that are set for our part of the covenant, we can see an aspect of the covenant that is conditional on our compliance. This conditional aspect of the covenant is characterized by "If . . . then . . . " clauses: *If* you will keep this covenant, *then* I will bless you. *If* you will be obedient children of God, *then* all will be well. This conditional aspect to the covenant suggests that our relationship with God depends to some extent on what we do. It suggests that in the Law there is a pattern that we are expected to follow. We can call it a pattern of behavior, a code of living, moral law, or whatever else we might choose to label it. The important point is that the articulation of the law implies that there are certain spiritual laws operating in this life, whether we recognize them or not.

But even though there were conditions spelled out for humankind in the developing covenant, there were also unconditional aspects to God's contract with us. These suggest that no matter how poorly we keep our end of the bargain, there are certain clauses in God's contract that He will honor no matter what we do. For example, when Israel finally enters the Promised Land, the people are reminded that they have not kept their part of the covenant and must therefore contend with enemies that will be allowed to remain in Canaan. But, at the same time, God reassures them that He will never break His covenant with them. This suggests that, even though the Israelites had to meet the consequences of their disharmony with the law, that did not cancel out the element of God's love that would never forsake them.

This reassurance is stated beautifully by King David on his deathbed. Aware that he had broken the covenant repeatedly, David nevertheless affirms, " . . . he hath made with me an everlasting covenant, ordered in all things, and sure: for this is all my salvation . . . " (II Samuel 23:5)

Perhaps the everlasting covenant David spoke of foreshadows one that Jeremiah prophesied when he said:

> Behold, the days come, saith the Lord, that I will make a new covenant with the house of Israel, and with the house of Judah: Not according to the covenant that I made with their fathers in the day that I took them by the hand to bring them out of the land of Egypt; which my covenant they brake, although I

was an husband unto them, saith the Lord: But this shall be the covenant that I will make with the house of Israel; After those days, saith the Lord, I will put my law in their inward parts, and write it in their hearts; and will be their God, and they shall be my people. And they shall teach no more every man his neighbour, and every man his brother, saying, Know the Lord: for they shall all know me, from the least of them unto the greatest of them, saith the Lord: for I will forgive their iniquity, and I will remember their sin no more. Jeremiah 31:31-34

This prophecy of a new covenant, in which the Law will be written on our hearts, suggests that a new order of relationship between God and humankind is being prepared. Under the old covenants people look to a set of rules and regulations, and if they followed them with the best of intentions and lived according to their precepts, they were taking the best path to reconciliation with God. We might say that under the rule of the old covenant people would be outwardly motivated.

The new covenant, on the other hand, promised an inward motivation, where the knowing to do right springs from within. This inward motivation would be quite a different experience from following a set of laws, even though the observable behavior may be the same in both cases. The difference is subtle, but it represents a quantum leap in the plan of reconciliation between God and humankind. It also represents the main difference between Old Testament and New, for these two portions of the Bible are the records of the old and new covenants, respectively.

If we look at the Bible as a whole, we may see it as the story of how the covenant that had to do with following a pattern of behavior and living cooperatively with the law of cause and effect gave way, developed, came into full blossom in the New Testament, or the new covenant.

For it is in the New Testament that the promised Messiah shows fully the love and mercy of God, His unconditional covenant with us, and that inward motivation that puts us in at-one-ment with our Creator.

In the Old and New Covenants, we once again pick up the two threads we can trace from Eden:

The Twin Threads Running Through the Plan of Salvation

In the first thread, the development of the plan of salvation may be traced through the following events and conditions:

Banishment from Eden

Lesson in Cause and Effect Comes with the Flood

Law Characterizes God's Relationship with Humankind

Conditional Covenant Requires Humankind's Obedience

Old Covenant Embodies All of the Above

Codes, Rules, Regulations Provide the Blueprint for Human Behavior

Outward or External Motivation Can Result in Righteousness

In the second thread, the development of the plan of salvation may be traced through the following events and conditions:

First Messianic Promise Given in Eden

First Covenant Is Established After the Flood

Mercy and Forgiveness Characterize God's Relationship with Humankind

Unconditional Covenant Promises God's Enduring Love, Despite Disobedience

New Covenant Embodies All of the Above

Law Written on Heart Prompts Appropriate Behavior

Inward or Internal Motivation Can Result in Righteousness

How does all of this relate to reincarnation and Christianity? The relationship can be made quite apparent simply by adding two more words to the lists above: karma and grace. The prevailing theme in the list on the left suggests that we are responsible for what we do. Karma would be a logical addition to such a list. The prevailing theme in the list at the right suggests that somehow, even though we don't deserve it, a way of mercy and forgiveness for the human soul has been in preparation for us since the time of the Fall. Grace clearly belongs at the head of this list.

Now, if we can reconcile these two lists of concepts, if we can take the two threads we have been tracing and twine them into a single, unified strand, we will have successfully integrated reincarnation and Christianity! For when we examine the concepts in these two columns of words, it becomes clear that the reconciliation of reincarnation with Christianity is nothing more and nothing less than the reconciliation of karma with grace, of old covenant with new. And, to add two New Testament concepts to our lists, the reconciliation of reincarnation with Christianity may be summed up as a matter of reconciling our works with our faith:

Reincarnation and the Intertwining of the Twin Threads

Karma	Grace
Banishment	Messianic Promise
Cause and Effect	First Covenant
Law	Mercy and Forgiveness
Conditional Covenant	Unconditional Covenant
Old Covenant (Testament)	New Covenant (Testament)
Codes, Rules, Regulations	Law Written on Heart
External Motivation	Internal Motivation
Works	Faith

An Exploration of Karma and Grace

Karma—the inexorable progression of cause and effect through a succession of human experiences; the doctrine that teaches we will sow what we reap, that we are responsible for our actions. If Christianity and the work of Christ are based not on karma but on grace, how can we reconcile the two? When an individual embraces a reincarnationist belief, is he or she, after all, renouncing the grace that is offered in Christ? If so, then maybe reincarnation and Christianity have no meeting ground. But if not, then perhaps it is possible for the reincarnationist and the nonreincarnationist to be united in a common state of grace. The answer may lie in a further exploration of grace.

Karma, because it is rational and logical, is fairly easy for us to understand. Even without a belief in karma, most people can easily understand the concept. Grace, on the other hand, is a far more challenging concept for the human mind to grasp. In fact, it would not be an exaggeration to say that grace is one of the great riddles of spiritual truth. As long as we try to understand it from the limited perspective of our vantage point here on this earth plane, we may never understand the full meaning of grace. The operation of grace in human life is certainly a mystery of unfathomable proportions.

But we are in good company if we sometimes feel that grace is a concept that escapes our understanding. We have evidence that even the apostle Paul, for all his faith and despite his immortal letters, did not understand the workings of grace. He admits as much in the opening of his first letter to the Corinthians. For in I Corinthians 1 this great teacher/preacher, who probably did more than any other single human being to spread the gospel throughout the world, is at a loss to explain to people just what it was that Jesus accomplished on the cross. In essence, he says, "I don't understand what really happened on Calvary. It's a mystery."

For example, Paul talks about the "foolishness" of the "preaching of the cross," emphasizing that grace is not to be grasped by rational principles; that, like all mysteries, it defies the logic of our temporal understanding.

> For the preaching of the cross is to them that perish foolishness; but unto us which are saved it is the power of God . . . For the Jews require a sign, and the Greeks seek after wisdom: But we preach Christ crucified, unto the Jews a stumblingblock, and unto the Greeks foolishness; But unto them which are called, both Jews and Greeks, Christ the power of God, and the wisdom of God. I Corinthians 1:18, 22-24

Paul's use of the words "foolishness" and "stumblingblock" underscore the ultimately irrational and mysterious nature of Christ's atonement and the grace it offered the human soul, as well as our predisposition to reject the incomprehensible. How we human beings hate to acknowledge that which shakes our comfortable suppositions about the way the world works! It's hard for us to live in the tension that results when we cannot neatly package an idea and logically understand it. We'd rather have the comfortable assurance that we understand something. It makes us feel more in control. Yet Paul's letter asks us to live in the state of tension that says, "I don't know quite how it works, but through the work of Christ there is a force in operation that can alter the destiny of the human soul."

While we may never completely comprehend grace, we can broaden our understanding of it when we look more closely at the central figure of Jesus. As the one through whom grace was made available to us, He is key to our understanding. Further, in the central figure of Jesus the Christ, we have the solution to the paradox of karma vs. grace. For, in examining the work of Jesus the Christ, we can discern the unifying principle that mediates between old covenant and new, tying together the two apparently diverse columns of words we have been developing:

Jesus, Mediator of the New Covenant

**Jesus the Christ
unifies the twin threads
running through the
plan of salvation**

Jesus the Christ

Jesus, the Pattern   *Jesus, the Atoner*

Karma	Grace
Banishment	Messianic Promise
Cause and Effect	First Covenant
Law	Mercy and Forgiveness
Conditional Covenant	Unconditional Covenant
Old Covenant (Testament)	New Covenant (Testament)
Codes, Rules, Regulations	Law Written on Heart
External Motivation	Internal Motivation
Works	Faith
Logical, Rational	Mysterious, Irrational

In both the Bible and the Edgar Cayce readings we can find some interesting descriptions of the role played by Jesus Christ in His making the way of salvation clear for us. Or, perhaps it would be more accurate to say *roles*, for we often hear Jesus' impact described in at least two rather distinct ways. Within the more doctrinally conservative Christian circles, we most often hear an emphasis on Jesus' role as atoner and savior. Within reincarnationist circles we most often hear an emphasis on Jesus' role of perfect pattern or example for us.

Which Jesus is the biblical one? It seems that both are. If we examine the scriptural record, we find that it presents Jesus in two roles. The same is true in the readings of Edgar Cayce. Both portraits depict an essential part of the work of Jesus Christ. Neither by itself is complete. It is only we who, looking through the window of our own biases, choose to emphasize one Jesus at the expense of the other.

Jesus the Pattern and Way-Shower. In His role of perfect pattern and way-shower, Jesus serves as the ultimate example for us to emulate. In Him we have the perfect manifestation of spirit in a material world. Because He is a pattern, we are expected to follow His lead, to do our best to model our lives after His, in spirit if not in specific circumstances. The word *forerunner* is used in the Bible to describe this role. For example, in Hebrews 6:20: " . . . the forerunner is for us entered [within the veil of the holy of holies], even Jesus." The entering in as a forerunner certainly ties in to the pattern role. In this context Jesus is one who blazes a trail so that others may follow in His footsteps.

There is another term frequently used in the Bible to describe Jesus as the pattern and way-shower. In numerous passages Jesus is called the "firstfruits," "first that should rise from the dead," and "the first begotten of the dead . . . " (see Acts 26:23, I Corinthians 15:20, Romans 8:29, Revelation 1:5) The use of the term *firstfruits* indicates that there will be additional fruits ripening after the first one. If Jesus the person is a firstfruit, it is only reasonable to conclude that the fruits to come will be those people who come after Him. Similarly, the descriptive phrase, "the first begotten of the dead," suggests that others are to follow in Jesus' path. Jesus' intention that we follow His example is nowhere more clearly indicated than in Hebrews 2:11, which tells us that He is not ashamed to call us brothers.

If we turn to the Edgar Cayce readings, we find that their references to Jesus as pattern and example are plentiful. In fact, such references are so plentiful that it will probably suffice to include just one excerpt that is representative of this entire collection of readings:

> For He hath not willed that any soul should perish, but hath given even His Son as the Pattern— yea, thy brother, Jesus, the Christ—that ye may know what is the way, what is the manner. For *He* is the way, *He* is the vine, and *He* abideth in the Father and ye as the branches abide in Him—as ye *do* His biddings. 1440-2

Clearly, the emphasis here is on heeding the perfect example of Jesus. From this reading we would conclude that Jesus is the "way" in that He lived the perfect life. That same perfect life, as a pattern for all souls, becomes the way for those who follow it.

In both the Bible and the Cayce readings, then, we can see emphasis on the importance of Jesus' example for us. A clear corollary to that emphasis is the behavior that we must exhibit in order to follow this example. Jesus in His role of way-shower/pattern may then be seen to fit the left-hand column of words, for it is consistent with the emphases of law, conditional covenant, and karma. As may be expected, Jesus' other role is most consistent with the words in the column on the right.

Jesus the Atoner/Power/Breakthrough. If the Bible speaks frequently of Jesus as the firstfruits, forerunner, and first begotten from the dead, it speaks just as often of Jesus as atoner for our sins. Now this is quite a different emphasis from that of pattern, for it suggests that, beyond showing us how to live, He interceded with God the Father and made restitution for our shortcomings. In so doing, He became the embodiment of the unconditional covenant, as it is under the terms of the unconditional covenant that we are reconciled with God in spite of, rather than because of, our behavior. In this context, we are looking at Jesus in His role of Savior. Just as the responsibility of following His example was a corollary to the Jesus-as-pattern role, the necessity of believing in (or accepting) the atonement He made for us is the corollary to Jesus-as-savior. Grace comes into operation when we believe, accept, or have faith in what Jesus accomplished on our behalf through His life, death, and resurrection.

While most of us have often heard the role of Jesus as savior expounded from Scripture, it may come as a surprise to many that the Edgar Cayce readings also brought this role to light. For example, as we saw in chapter 11:

> Hence the shedding of the blood in the *man* Jesus made for the atoning for *all* men, through making Himself in at-onement with the law and with love . . . in the . . . shedding of the blood comes the redemption to man . . . 262-45

And in another reading:

In the blood of the Christ as was shed karma is met and then it becomes the law, not of cause and effect, but of being justified by faith in Him. 2828-5

Expressing this truth most succinctly of all is the reading that states:

He is thy *karma,* if ye put thy trust *wholly* in Him! 2067-2

These excerpts strongly imply that, from the perspective of the Cayce readings, Jesus did more than just show us the way. He was more than a good man or even a perfect man. He made a breakthrough for us. He accomplished something on the soul level that made it forever different for people who came after Him and also for people who lived before Him. He made it possible for the prophecy of Jeremiah to be fulfilled. For, somewhere at the core of the mystery of grace is the promise that the law *can* be written on our hearts, through no special merit of our own.

We can now see two sets of concepts converging on a central issue: How can it be true that Jesus came to show us the way to live and yet also came to accomplish something that all our efforts to follow His example could never have produced on their own? How do we meet our obligation to obey God in the way we live our lives, and yet at the same time trust in Jesus for our salvation? These questions are all contained in a controversy that rages through the pages of the New Testament: Are we saved by our faith or by our works?

If we can resolve this question, we will have reconciled reincarnation with Christianity. After all, the main Christian objection to reincarnation is that it is a doctrine of salvation by works that ignores the saving power of Jesus. But if faith and works can be seen as compatible components in a Christian's belief system, so then can karma and grace coexist without violation of essential Christian faith.

The Ultimate Unity of Karma and Grace

Perhaps we can best understand the compatibility of karma and grace by looking at an analogy. Suppose you are in the center of a maze, and your job is to get out. Now there are two ways that you can go about getting through your maze. You can blindly fumble and bumble your way down the various corridors. When you hit a dead end, you must go back and retrace your steps to the point where you made the wrong turn, then try once again to make the right turn. Sometimes you might happen to make the right choice on the first try. But then the next thing you know, you've run into another blank wall. Once more you must retrace your steps and correct the wrong turn. This path of trial and error would be like taking the way of karma (or law or works).

Suppose, on the other hand, that someone said to you, "I've successfully completed that maze, and I have a map that shows every turn. Furthermore, if you'll accept my map, I'll impart to you the strength and the wisdom you need to follow my map. You may not understand how I can give you this special help, but if you will just accept it, you will experience it working on your trip through the maze. You will succeed, not through your own efforts, but by trusting that I have already secured your release from this maze." This would be like the way of grace: accepting the map—which would be analogous to Jesus as the pattern—and accepting the power to follow the map. Accepting the power would be like accepting Jesus' role of breakthrough for us, Jesus as atoner.

Now, accepting the map would not mean that it was no longer important to make the correct turns in the maze or that the corridors would be miraculously altered to allow your free passage. Instead, the map would be the best and most efficient means of making the correct turns in the first place. To translate this out of the maze analogy and back into our original terminology, under grace you would necessarily also conform to the laws of karma. Your actions, your behavior would be consistent with what the law required. The law would have been fulfilled, even though you were not directly "following" the path of law.

We can trace this same development of thought through the New Testament period, when a much-debated issue was the question of whether the people newly converted to the Christian faith were obligated to keep what we know today as Old Testament law. For example, consider the many passages which report arguments over whether it was necessary for Gentile Christians to be circumcised. Circumcision for the Jew was representative of being bound by the Law. Were the Gentile Christians also taking on responsibility to keep the Law when they joined the new Jewish sect that followed Jesus? Or were they totally free to disregard the Law?

Jesus seemed to sum up the sometimes bewildering relationship between old covenant (characterized by Law) and new covenant (characterized by grace) when He said, "l am not come to destroy [the law], but to fulfill [it]." (Matthew 5:17) What is fulfilling the law if not living it perfectly? Yet in living it perfectly, Jesus was clearly not bound by the "rules and regulations" aspect of it. He healed on the Sabbath, for example. In keeping the perfect *spirit* or motivation of the law, Jesus did indeed fulfill the prophecy of Jeremiah which spoke of a law that would be written on the heart.

The law written on the heart makes one do right from an inner motivation rather than because certain actions are dictated by code. This inward motivation is one characteristic of living under the law of grace. It is a state of being that we must *choose,* however. Thus, the Christian reincarnationist may believe that there is such a thing as karma, just as the nonreincarnationist Christian believes that there is such a thing as Old Testament law. But the fundamental Christian is bound neither to Old Testament law nor to karma if he chooses instead the state of grace offered in Jesus.

We can see this relationship between law and grace—or works and faith—explained much the same way in the Bible. Both are important. In fact, they are inseparable. Yet, just as we saw how one role of Jesus is sometimes featured at the expense of obscuring the other, sometimes either faith or works can be highlighted in such a way that the other side of the coin is lost. For example, there are certain Bible verses that have become the cornerstone of belief for Christian denominations that stress salvation solely through faith in Jesus. At the extreme, the doctrines of these denominations hold that our behavior has no bearing on our soul's destiny, that faith alone will determine our eternal fate. Under such a belief system, it would not matter if a person lived a loving, good life. Even the purest of humans are still so sinful that without faith in Jesus they are lost forever, some Christians believe. By the same token, you could believe in Jesus and make lots of mistakes—maybe even live a life clearly less pure than that of your non-Christian neighbor—and still be saved on the basis of your faith alone.

Such beliefs are based on such Scriptures as:

For God so loved the world, that he gave his only begotten Son, that whosoever believeth in Him should not perish, but have everlasting life. John 3:16

Or:

> . . . by grace are ye saved through faith; and that not of yourselves: it is the gift of God: Not of works, lest any man should boast. Ephesians 2:8-9

Such verses may seem to make a clearcut case for salvation by faith alone, and yet there are others that suggest that there is another side to the coin.

From the book of Romans, for example, we have a somewhat different idea:

> [God] will render to every man according to his deeds: To them who by patient continuance in well doing seek for glory and honour and immortality, eternal life: But unto them that are contentious, and do not obey the truth, but obey unrighteousness, indignation and wrath, Tribulation and anguish, upon every soul of man that doeth evil, of the Jew first, and also of the Gentile . . . Romans 2:6-9

This passage and others like it would seem to indicate that not only does our behavior count, but that right living has a part in winning us eternal life.

These two contrasting passages from Ephesians and from Romans are representative of many more similar passages. Some biblical texts seem to say that we are saved by faith and others seem to say we are saved by our works or by the way we live. Do we have a contradiction within the pages of New Testament Scripture, or have we once again come up against a paradox, in which two seemingly irreconcilable opposites are both true at the same time? Further scriptural evidence favors our understanding this apparent contradiction as paradox, as James so expertly demonstrates in the second chapter of his epistle. Here we find a treatment of the knotty problem of faith vs. works which shows the ultimate unity between the two. Let's follow the logic of James's argument. He begins by getting right at the crux of the controversy: "What doth it profit, my brethren, though a man say he hath faith, and have not works? can faith save him?" (verse 14)

Obviously James is addressing the very question we have been pondering: Is it belief alone that saves us? In answer to this, James uses a concrete illustration to point out the emptiness of a professed faith which is not borne out in one's behavior:

> If a brother or sister be naked, and destitute of daily food, And one of you say unto them, Depart in peace, be ye warmed and filled; notwithstanding ye give them not those things which are needful to the body; what doth it profit? Even so faith, if it hath not works, is dead, being alone. Verses 15-17

James is stating unequivocally that it is not good enough to offer our best wishes if we do nothing to actually help our needy brothers. Drawing a parallel between such empty "good will" and empty faith, James goes on to build a case for the inseparability of true faith from works:

> Yea, a man may say, Thou hast faith, and I have works; show me thy faith without thy works, and I will show thee my faith by my works. Verse 18

The salient point here is that as we follow Jesus' example or live cooperatively with the law, we are also living our faith completely. Conversely, if we are truly living our faith, the works or appropriate behavior automatically follows. James emphasizes this point when he says:

> Thou believest that there is one God; thou doest well: the devils also believe, and tremble. But wilt

thou know, O vain man, that faith without works is dead?" Verses 19-20

Finally, using examples from the Old Testament record, James insists that the work of obeying God's will entails an act of faith and that if we truly believe, our actions must reflect this:

Was not Abraham our father justified by works, when he had offered Isaac his son upon the altar? Verse 21

Now this is an interesting example to consider. Abraham's near sacrifice of Isaac is traditionally held up as an example of supreme faith. Abraham's faith in God was so great that he was willing to put his son on the altar. Yet James says, "Was not Abraham . . . justified by *works . . .* " The point James seems to be trying to emphasize is that in the very act of being willing to lay his son on the altar, Abraham was *doing* something that demonstrated his faith. We might rephrase this and conclude that as we live out our faith, the keeping of the law is a necessary byproduct.

This point is made further in the next verses:

Seest thou how faith wrought with his works, and by works was faith made perfect? And the scripture was fulfilled which saith, Abraham believed God, and it was imputed unto him for righteousness: and he was called the Friend of God. Verse 23

We can see here the cyclic relationship of faith and works. Faith motivated Abraham's actions in the first place, but those works were then required to make Abraham's faith perfect.

James goes on to conclude his discourse:

Ye see then how that by works a man is justified, and not by faith only. Likewise also was not Rahab the harlot justified by works, when she had received the messengers, and had sent them out another way? For as the body without the spirit is dead, so faith without works is dead also. Verses 24-26

We can see, then, that the apparent conflict between faith and works was no conflict at all. Faith and works are merely two sides of the same coin. One cannot exist without the other. Not only does James's discourse demonstrate the ultimate unity of faith and works, but it also shows that the old covenant and the new, Jesus the Pattern and Jesus the Atoner, are also one. Indeed, the concepts (in the two columns) we have been tracing from their inception in the Eden story are in reality just two sides to the same coin.

What does this suggest for the Christian reincarnationist? It suggests that when someone of the Christian faith asserts that belief in reincarnation precludes the possibility of being a "true" Christian, perhaps that individual has not fully considered the relationship of faith and works. For the reincarnationist's job of harmonizing karmic law with the work of Christ is no greater than the nonreincarnationist's job of harmonizing saving faith with the concomitant responsibility to reflect that faith in his or behavior.

The secret of the new Covenant is that true faith and true compliance with the pattern of the law—be it karmic or Old Testament—are one. Grace, then, is the living principle which allows reconciliation with God and which fulfills the law. For the Christian reincarnationist and the nonreincarnationist Christian, the basic issues are the same. In both lines of belief we have a responsibility before God to live in harmony with certain behavioral requirements. The desired end in both lines of belief is reunion with God. For reincarnationist and nonreincarnationist Christians alike, grace is the transcendent principle which transforms lives and returns us to the Father. But what of this return to the Father? To address the last of the Christian objections to reincarnation which we have identified, does this return preclude the possibility of a resurrected body?

Reincarnation and the Resurrected Body

I have already stated that not all (and probably not even many) reincarnationists believe that a resurrected physical body is part of the soul's ultimate reunion with the Father. I will not pretend that the bodily resurrection is a standard aspect of the reincarnationist philosophy. *But for those who do believe the doctrine of bodily resurrection,* is there any way that we can understand this event in the light of the reincarnationist scenario for the soul? The key, it would seem, is in taking a closer look at the nature of the resurrected body.

What Is the Resurrection of the Body? Perhaps one of the most unpleasant facts of life is that the physical body is destined to decay once the life has gone out of it. No believer in the bodily resurrection would claim, I'm sure, that the specific atoms and molecules that made up believer John Smith while he lived on this earth 100 years ago are being preserved in the grave, awaiting the bodily resurrection. To the contrary, the real miracle of the bodily resurrection is that somehow John Smith will be "reconstructed," the atoms and molecules being once again arranged into a pattern that is recognizable as John Smith. In essence, John Smith will be made by God all over again, according to the blueprint for the perfect John Smith.

This process bears some striking similarities to the process by which the soul takes on each physical incarnation under the reincarnation philosophy. It is a gross oversimplification and distortion of the reincarnation process to portray it in terms of the soul merely "entering" body after body in its quest for perfection. The relationship between body and soul is actually much closer than that, and it can be understood best in terms of the "blueprint" concept introduced above. For the sake of illustration, let's consider the following description of the reincarnation process:

Incarnation: Soul Pattern Taking on Physical Form. Each of us, on the soul level, is a nonphysical being. It is the nonphysical part of us that survives bodily death and that carries a continuous identity from lifetime to lifetime. We might say that it is the nonphysical part of us that carries the blueprint for the way we will manifest in a material world, i.e., the physical body. At any given time, that nonphysical part of us represents the composite of everything we have ever done or experienced in our collection of lives on the earth. It's not so much that we take on a "different" body every time we incarnate, but rather that we draw to ourselves the physical form that best reflects our continuous soul identity at that particular time. It might work something like this:

If we imagine that our nonphysical identity, in its capacity to grow and change as we grow and change, may be likened to a piece of clay, we can begin to see how our choices shape our identity. With each choice we make, through our varied experiences in the earth, that "claylike" nonmaterial identity is shaped, bearing the results of each experience. A talent developed here, a problem dwelled on there, a happy experience, a painful one— they each leave their mark on that inner identity. From lifetime to lifetime, that unique structure of our inner identity serves as the blueprint that shapes the form of our manifestation through a physical body.

To take the illustration a step further in showing how this might come about, imagine that that inner identity is like a magnet. Just as a magnet will draw iron filings to itself, the filings clinging to and covering the magnet until it is completely encased, our inner identity, our own blueprint, draws to itself the genetic and environmental factors that adequately reflect that inner pattern. The outer, physical form fits hand-in-glove with the inner identity.

Thus, though we may go through many incarnations, each appearance is really just another arrangement of atoms and molecules around the same soul identity. Yes, that soul pattern may make substantial changes from lifetime to lifetime, but then don't people sometimes do the same within the course of one lifetime? When one asks "which body" the reincarnationist would occupy in the bodily resurrection, it is analogous to asking the nonreincarnationist whether one will occupy the two-year-old or the fifty-year-old version of one's earthly body. The question is fallacious, because according to the doctrine of the bodily resurrection, we will each occupy the *ideal* version of the body we have had in this life. Just so with the Christian reincarnationist; the body he or she will occupy in the resurrection would be an arrangement of atoms and molecules according to the ideal pattern for that particular soul. It would be a perfect composite version of all the physical forms that soul may ever have manifested.

The bodily resurrection, like the other fundamental Christian doctrines we have considered, does not present an irreconcilable problem for the reincarnationist. Instead, couldn't we see reincarnation as a viable—but optional—component of Christian faith?

Reincarnation as an Option Within Christian Faith

Reincarnation is not the gospel. It is not a doctrine that one must embrace in order to be redeemed or re-united with the Father. Reincarnation is by no means an essential component of Christian faith. But its explanation of some of life's puzzles may make it a tenable option for the Christian. As long as reincarnation is compatible with the central message of traditional Christianity, that our salvation or reconciliation with the Father is a gift made possible in Jesus, and that we do not earn our salvation by following a set of rules and regulations, there is no reason that one might not be both a reincarnationist and a fundamental Christian.

Whether we speak the language of reincarnation or Evangelical Christianity, our charge is to "put on Christ," trusting in His power to transform the soul, and then living in such a way that His presence is apparent in our lives. In so doing, every "jot and tittle" of the law, every condition of the law of karma, will be fulfilled. Is this not in line with what Jesus' ministry was all about?

Part
Five

Edgar Cayce and the Bible

15

The Edgar Cayce Readings
and Bible Interpretation

THE STRONG BIBLICAL flavor of the Cayce readings is apparent to even the most casual observer. Not only do we find an abundance of biblical quotes and paraphrases, but the very language in which Cayce spoke while giving his readings echoes the language of the Bible he knew so well. It is not unusual, for example, to find frequent use of the archaic "thee's" and "thou's" of the King James Version, even in health readings.

Cayce enthusiasts will sometimes point to the biblical tone of his readings as evidence that their message is indeed compatible with the Bible. Some skeptical Christians are unconvinced by this reasoning. They will respond with the "counterfeit" argument discussed in chapter 7, whereby the readings' very similarity to the Bible becomes evidence for Satanic treachery. Of course, the readings appear to be like the Bible on the surface, their argument goes. How else would Satan go about deceiving people into accepting the Cayce material as God centered?

In one sense it is true that the Bible quotes, paraphrases, and biblical language in the readings do not prove their authenticity as a source of spiritually accurate information. From a purely psychological perspective, we can trace the preponderance of biblical material in Edgar Cayce's readings to his conscious preoccupation with the Bible. We know that from his boyhood Edgar Cayce read the Bible regularly and avidly. We know that his commitment to it led him to a practice no less ambitious than reading it from cover to cover once for every year of his life. We know that Edgar Cayce the man was a Sunday school teacher, and apparently a gifted one. And we are told by those who knew him best that he turned first to his Bible in times of personal trouble. In short, we know that Cayce's conscious mind was saturated with the Bible.

Just a rudimentary understanding of psychology will suggest that Cayce's unconscious mind was also saturated with his conscious Bible reading and study. It would be no surprise, then, to see evidence of that biblical orientation in his readings. Even the best psychic, after all, must funnel information through his or her own mind. There is no such thing as "pure" psychic information, as long as that information is mediated through the consciousness of a human being. To see how this is true, we might consider the following analogy: Suppose we took a paper coffee filter and saturated it with ink. When we put this filter into a coffee maker, the ink would color any liquid that was poured through it. Even if we started with perfectly clear water, we would get tinged water once it had passed through that filter. If the water we poured through was murky to begin with, the ink would only further muddy the water.

The minds of psychics are like those filters. Some psychics will be relatively clear channels, picking up clear (or true) information to begin with and giving it a minimum of their own distortion as it passes through their unconscious minds. Others may not be as reliable, picking up muddied information in the first place and/ or adding so much of their own distortion when verbalizing the information that it becomes difficult to sort out.

Of course, the job of sorting out psychic information is ultimately one that each individual must undertake. Accuracy in the factual sense is something that must be determined through impartial evaluation of empirical results. Accuracy in the spiritual sense—for the person of biblically centered Christian faith at least—must be evaluated according to the two main principles discussed in chapters 7 and 8: the spiritual integrity of the source and whether it leads people toward or away from faith in Christ. When it comes to evaluating Cayce as a psychic source, then, his readings' treatment of the Bible is a very important factor to consider. The fact that the readings bear many similarities to the Bible is not enough. The *real* issue lies in what these readings say about the Bible and its message for us.

In order to evaluate the readings' message concerning the Bible, we must examine their basic approach to biblical interpretation. Often Cayce's detractors accuse his readings of taking a twisted and inappropriate interpretation of Scripture to support their own unorthodox "teachings." Are there any grounds for these charges? That question can only be answered after we have seen what the readings of Edgar Cayce actually say about Bible interpretation.

The Controversy over Bible Interpretation

Whenever we address the question of how best to interpret the Bible, we touch an area that can be controversial indeed. There are those who take the stand that the Bible is the literal, historical word of God and that any interpretation other than the literal is faulty and deceptive. On the other end of the spectrum, there are those who hold that it is naive to take a literal view of the Bible. Its tales of the miraculous fly in the face of modern science, they assert. At best, the Bible is a collection of myths that carry sociological significance, the extreme antiliteralists would claim.

Of course, there are countless positions that fall somewhere between these two ends of the spectrum. For example, the majority of even fundamental Christians, while holding to literal interpretation as a rule, allow for allegory and the acceptability of symbolic interpretation within limitations. Certain circumscribed portions of Scripture, such as the Book of the Revelation or the Song of Solomon, would be acceptable places to interpret symbolically for these more moderate literalists. There is similar moderation among many who generally take a nonliteral view. Even among these nonliteralists, there is often a tendency to take certain scriptural reports as literal. For example, one who took the resurrection to be an allegorical story might still see the crucifixion as a literal event.

When it comes to Bible interpretation, then, there are many intermediate positions along the literalist-nonliteralist scale. Commitment to the correctness of one's own position and the incorrectness of other positions usually runs fairly strong!

Where do the Edgar Cayce readings stand with respect to this controversy? Can we put them in the camp of the literalists or can we put them in the camp of the nonliteralists? The thousands of Cayce readings that touch on the Bible can lead to only one conclusion: These readings affirm the validity of *both* the literal and the nonliteral approaches to Bible interpretation. In fact, these readings seem to suggest that there are no less than three levels of Bible interpretation that, when taken as a whole, give us a complete view of the Bible's message for us. Heresy? Before any of my readers jump to that conclusion, let's take time to look at what these three levels are. For in the readings' treatment of the literal, symbolic, and practical levels of Bible interpretation, I believe we have a form of biblical exegesis that stands up to the most critical Christian scrutiny.

The Bible as Literal, Historical Word of God

When we think about Edgar Cayce the psychic, Edgar Cayce the man who did so much to reintroduce reincarnation into Western thinking, Edgar Cayce the object of so much Christian criticism, we might not realize that this same Edgar Cayce was a great champion of a very traditional view of the Bible; that is, the view that the Bible is indeed the inspired, reliable record of God's dealings with humankind.

To fully appreciate this we must remember that Cayce came along at a time when it was becoming theologically fashionable to deny the miraculous and supernatural in the Bible. Around the turn of the century, a number of theories were developed to "explain" the supernatural events of the Bible in terms of natural law. The most well known, of course, is the postulation that Jesus did not actually die on the cross and resurrect: He was merely in a coma from which he emerged after being laid in the tomb. Other miracles were explained away with alternate interpretations of the biblical text. At the feeding of the five thousand, for example, the "miracle" lay in the fact that Jesus so inspired people with love that they shared food that they had brought with them stashed up their sleeves. For some modern Christians, the miracles of Jesus became an embarrassment, something that made their faith untenable in the face of twentieth-century science.

Yet Cayce spoke clearly and unashamedly of the miraculous in the Bible. Through the pages of hundreds of readings given about Bible times or about people who lived in those times, we see what amounts to eyewitness accounts of biblical events that might try the credibility of the materially oriented reader. The virgin birth of Jesus, His power to heal and perform other miracles, even His resurrection, are all covered with a matter-of-factness that implies such events are natural indeed where God is concerned!

Edgar Cayce Treats the Miraculous as Factual. In scanning the pages of various Cayce readings that deal with biblical events, we can find reference to many of the miraculous and rather spectacular events reported in Scripture. Nowhere do we find the Cayce source explaining away or denying the miraculous. Instead, we find the miraculous nature of those events taken as a given, something so completely accepted that the readings do not even bother to defend or explain it.

To illustrate this point, let's consider one representative case: the story of the battle of Jericho. Now this is one portion of the Bible that we might be inclined to doubt as literal truth, if we were to go through Scripture demythologizing, or reinterpreting, those events that would seem to defy natural law and common reason. After all, the Bible tells us in this story (Joshua, chapter 6) that Israel, even though outnumbered, takes the mighty, walled city of Jericho just by marching around it and sounding the trumpet. The nonliteralist might well decide to view this as a symbolic story rather than deal with the problems it presents for the rational, scientific mind. Yet Edgar Cayce dealt with this story as literal truth. At least two people were told in their life readings that they were present at Jericho. In the way these readings refer to the events that took place there, it is clear that a literal interpretation of the story is assumed.

The first person was told that he was among the Israelites who were born during the forty-year period when Israel wandered in the wilderness, after leaving Egypt but before entering the Promised Land. The reading says that "The entity then was in the families of Aaron or the tribe of Levi; not a high priest but a lesser priest to whom there was given the mission of sounding the call to worship . . . " (3183-1)

We are looking, then, at the story of a relatively low-ranking priest who had the job of sounding the horn to call the people together for worship. The account goes on, in speaking about this trumpeter-priest, to say that he was one who "led those groups about Jericho; being among the first to enter that fallen city. This has ever been a favorite story of the entity . . . the trumpet has ever been a favorite instrument but the reed will bring . . . a greater accord or attunement . . . " (3183-1)

Before making note of the specific insights this reading has to offer, let's go on to consider another reading given to someone who was told he was at Jericho in a past life. This reading adds quite a different perspective on the story, because it was given for someone who was on the other side of the fence—literally. This individual was on the *inside* when the walls came down, and he apparently carries quite a different subconscious memory of the event. His reading said that he was "in that land when there was the return of the peoples to the Promised Land from exile . . . The entity then [was] in the name Rahai, and the entity was among those who defended the walls in Jericho when it came down, and the entity has in the present experience that innate feeling as regarding the Children of Promise, see?" (2734-1)

Now as we look at these two accounts, there are a number of things that may be noted. First, we should notice the passing references to key aspects of the biblical story of Jericho—the trumpet, the marching around the walls, the walls falling, etc. These references can only be seen as the natural outgrowth of the assumption that the fall of Jericho literally happened as reported in the Bible. There is no attempt to explain them away in allegorical terms.

These two readings also indicate some of the ways that events from the distant past might relate to people today. In the first case, the personal insights are admittedly not earth-shaking. The man is told why he always enjoyed the story of Jericho and is given an understanding of his liking for the trumpet. He's also given some practical advice concerning the reed instruments' capacity for awakening a different set of characteristics within him. But in the second case, this individual is told that because he was among the conquered people at Jericho, he has never forgiven the Jewish people. That must have been quite a revelation for him. We could imagine that it might have seemed just a little bit absurd to him that he was carrying a grudge against the descendants of those who had conquered his people in another lifetime! And we can hope that this was a first step for him in releasing a long-held prejudice.

By extension, we can see from just these two case histories that, from the viewpoint of the Cayce readings, the literal truth of the Bible is very important. Not only do the readings concur again and again with the historical veracity of the Bible, but they underline the importance of literal and historical interpretation of the Bible. For these readings make it clear that we are dealing with a

God who is active in history. That is, our God is not an impersonal force, aloof and uninvolved in the affairs of humankind. He is a God who intercedes, who is an active partner in His relationship with His children. We can learn and grow in our relationship with Him, then, as we study the record of His past dealings with mankind.

Can We Validate Edgar Cayce's Accounts of Biblical Events? At this point a question naturally arises: How could Cayce have obtained information on biblical events? Was he *really* seeing the battle of Jericho or was this just the product of an active and rather religious imagination? Particularly if we think back to the filter analogy discussed earlier in this chapter, we might attribute the readings' apparent substantiation of the literal biblical record to the natural influence of Cayce's conscious biases.

On one level, this may seem like an unnecessary question, since we are evaluating Edgar Cayce in terms of his compatibility with the more conservative versions of Christian belief concerning the Bible. It may be enough merely to demonstrate that his readings uphold the literal truth of the Bible and leave the question of whether those readings are objectively true to the nonliteralists. Nonetheless, it is an important point to consider, as it adds to our feeling for Cayce's veracity, first as a psychic source and secondly as a source of information related to the Bible.

Of course, there is ultimately no proof concerning Cayce's Bible readings. The best we can do is make a reasoned (and admittedly personal) decision concerning the readings' veracity, based on the evidence at hand. Edgar Cayce's overall accuracy on matters that could be verified is one important factor to weigh. The fact that his accuracy was so frequently confirmed when he gave physical diagnoses, for example, tends to add credence when we consider other types of readings not so easily verified.

But we need not look as far away as the health readings to find evidence that Cayce tended to be correct when he spoke of Bible history. Consider his uncanny anticipation of what scholars were later to discover with respect to the Essene sect of Jews. Students of the Cayce readings will know that this material speaks at length about the Essene sect, describing their activities, beliefs, and active preparation for the coming of the Messiah. In a reading given in 1937, Edgar Cayce described an Essene community "on the way above Emmaus to the way that 'goeth down towards Jericho' . . . " (1391-1) At this time scholars knew of no such community in that area. Yet ten years later—and two years after Edgar Cayce's death—archaeological explorations did indeed uncover an Essene community just where Cayce described its location.

Furthermore, in those Cayce readings that spoke about the Essenes, there was much information concerning the women of that community and their key roles in the activities of the sect. Scholars of Edgar Cayce's day were quite certain that the Essenes were a monastic community and, therefore, would have had no female members. Yet excavations of this Essene community referred to by Cayce revealed that over one-third of the skeletons were those of women!

It seems reasonable, then, for us at least tentatively to consider that Edgar Cayce may have been truly tapping an accurate record when his readings spoke so matter-of-factly concerning biblical events. Certainly for the individual already convinced of Edgar Cayce's accuracy, his readings on the Bible become a substantiation of the historical validity of Scripture.

The Readings Bring Out the Inspirational Value of the Literal. There is still another valuable aspect to the Cayce readings that focus on the literal level of Bible interpretation: These readings can hold a tremendous inspirational power. Too often, we can become so used to the wonderful stories in the Bible that we stop feeling their impact. While this may not be a problem for the person of newly found faith, the veteran church- and Sunday school-goer may find it all too easy to slip into a kind of complacence that blocks full appreciation of the familiar Bible stories. We can become so used to hearing these stories told, that we actually stop *hearing* them. If we're not careful, we may find ourselves daydreaming while some of those Bible stories are read to us in church, or reading words without feeling their meaning when we sit down with our Bibles.

This is probably why we have four Gospels—the same basic story is told from four perspectives that are just different enough to give the variety that the human mind demands: from Matthew, the perspective of one concerned with the fulfillment of Old Testament prophecies; from John, the more mystical emphasis, and so on. In the Cayce readings on biblical events, we have still another perspective on the well-known Bible stories. In telling the old familiar Bible stories in a new way, these readings make them come alive all over again.

An Account of the Last Supper. There is probably no better example of this ability to make biblical events come alive than reading 5749-1, which gives us an account of the Last Supper. This was an unusual reading, because it was unsolicited. On June 14, 1932, Edgar Cayce gave a check physical reading for a woman who had been receiving health advice. When he finished with this reading and was given the usual suggestion to awaken, there was no response. Two more times the suggestion to awaken was given, each time to no avail. Then, still in his sleeplike state, Cayce began to speak:

> The Lord's Supper—here with the Master—see what they had for supper—boiled fish, rice, with leeks, wine, and loaf. One of the pitchers in which it was served was broken—the handle was broken, as was the lip to same. 5749-1

Notice the detail that Cayce picks up on. We almost get the impression that he is witnessing this scene like the proverbial mouse in the corner, reporting back to us all that unfolds in the Upper Room. The report goes on to give us physical descriptions of Jesus' disciples, describing their clothing, coloring, and general manner. Then comes a description of Jesus Himself:

> The Master's hair is 'most red, inclined to be curly in portions, yet not feminine or weak—*strong*, with heavy piercing eyes that are blue or steel-gray.
> His weight would be at least a hundred and seventy pounds. Long tapering fingers, nails well kept. Long nail, though, on the left little finger.

In the midst of his account, Cayce has slipped into the present tense. We can imagine that the scene before his mind's eye has become so vivid that it truly seems to be happening moment by moment as he tells it.

We get a rather unusual portrait of Jesus' personality, too, for the reading tells us that He is merry at that last feast with His disciples and that He is joking with them, even as Judas is preparing to betray Him. The reading goes on to tell of the famous ceremony of the washing of the feet:

> Lays aside His robe, which is all of one piece—

girds the towel about His waist, which is dressed with linen that is blue and white. Rolls back the folds, kneels first before John, James, then to Peter—who refuses.

Then the dissertation as to "He that would be the greatest would be servant of all."

The robe referred to at the beginning of this excerpt is an object of interest, for it sheds some light on our understanding of Jesus' relationships with those who loved Him. Earlier in this reading we are told that this garment was given to Jesus by Nicodemus, and in other Cayce readings we are told that Nicodemus's wife had woven this seamless robe especially for Jesus. The robe was something treasured by Jesus and was apparently the same one for which the Roman soldiers gambled while He was on the cross.

It is also interesting to note how the reading goes into great detail concerning events not spelled out in the biblical account, yet makes no attempt to repeat those that are already reported for us in Scripture. This is particularly evident in the way the commentary simply says, "Then the dissertation as to 'He that would be the greatest . . . '" It may be inferred here that all of Cayce's listeners are expected to *know* the substance of that dissertation.

Following along to the conclusion of this reading, we are told that the little group then joins together in singing the 91st Psalm and that Jesus "is the musician as well, for He uses the harp." The reading then concludes as suddenly as it began: "They leave for the garden."

Now as we look at this account, a couple of observations can be made. First, it should be noted that Edgar Cayce did not offer his version of the Last Supper as a correction of the biblical account. Nowhere do we find a contradiction of what we have already had reported in Scripture. What we *do* find, however, is the addition of some details that give us a fuller picture of that momentous evening.

We did not have physical descriptions of Jesus and His disciples in the biblical account, nor did we have the information that Jesus played a harp. Yet none of this stands in conflict with the scriptural account. The merry and joking Jesus is not an image that we are used to encountering, yet it would seem that a sense of humor *would* be one characteristic of God-made-manifest-in-man. While these various details may not be essential to our knowledge of Jesus or our belief in Him, they have the effect of "fleshing out" our mental picture of Him, bringing Him that much closer to our awareness and making our faith that much more concrete. We might liken this effect to that of a quality biblical drama—in helping to make the Bible story come alive, it inspires us and turns us back to the original source with renewed commitment.

The evidence is clear, then, that the Cayce readings' approach to Bible interpretation is firmly rooted in the literal. Yet those same readings speak just as eloquently of a second level of interpretation, that of the symbolic.

The Symbolic Level of Bible Interpretation

The symbolic approach to interpreting the Bible often holds a particular allure for people of a metaphysical bent. For them, the symbolic carries the promise of unlocking hidden meanings and offering a greater depth of understanding. For those of a more conservative Christian persuasion, however, symbolic interpretation of the Bible carries an insidious danger. They charge that when we interpret the Bible symbolically, we can twist it to suit our own purposes and, therefore, easily fall into deception. This is a crucial point, one that must be adequately addressed when we attempt to harmonize the Cayce readings with biblically centered Christianity. When the readings encouraged a symbolic view of the Bible, were they opening the way for a random and subjective interpretation of Scripture? Let's find out by examining more closely the symbolic approach we find in these readings.

The People in the Bible Symbolize States of Human Consciousness. The basic principle of symbolic interpretation found in the Cayce readings suggests that we can view Bible characters as allegorical representations of our own inner traits. Abraham, for example, is symbolic of the kind of faith that responds to God's calling, according to the readings. (2174-2) Now if we consider the story of the literal Abraham and see how he left the only home and security he had ever known and ventured into a virtual wilderness on the basis of a call from God, it is not hard to see faith in action. It does not take a particularly esoteric approach to interpret Abraham as a symbol of faith. On the contrary, the symbolic interpretation is a natural outgrowth of what the literal story tells us about this character.

The value of symbolic interpretation becomes apparent when we consider how the story of Abraham could help each of us understand our own faith. For when we read about Abraham, not only do we have the story of the patriarch from thousands of years ago, but we also have the story of our own faith. In Abraham's strengths and weaknesses, and in the way he responded to the various experiences he encountered in life, we can gain insights concerning our own faith.

Israel, more broadly speaking, is symbolic of the seeker after truth, the readings tell us. (5377-1) A symbolic insight like this can unlock the meaning of the entire Old Testament drama for today's seeker. For in the literal story of the nation of Israel, each modern reader can learn much about the search for truth. We can all read of Israel's times of living in harmony and obedience with God's laws; we can read of their repeated rebellions and "stiff-necked" attitudes; and in this we can see reflections of our own search for truth. This perspective underscores the relationship between the Bible and people's individual souls. It emphasizes the Bible's import in our lives today, for from every event reported in the Bible, we can draw a symbolic interpretation of what that account has to teach us about our own hearts and minds.

Consider, for example, the symbolic significance of the Bethlehem manger scene. The readings of Edgar Cayce suggest that the three Wise Men and the gifts they brought were symbolic of body, mind, and soul. (5749-7) With this understanding, we can see that not only does the Bible report on that historical event from 2,000 years ago, but on a symbolic level it also gives us a reminder that body, mind, and soul are to bow before the Christ when He is born in our hearts.

Symbolic Interpretation Should Not Become a Mental Exercise. Working with symbols can be fun. There is for many of us a certain intellectual satisfaction in figuring out the symbolic message of a poem, a story, or even the Bible itself. Therein lies the danger. To the extent that we engage in symbolic interpretation as a mind game or in order to feel that our understanding is deeper than that of the strict literalist, we walk on shaky ground. Knowledge not lived is sin, the Cayce readings disconcertingly insist. (3428-1) In other words, we are responsible to act according to what we know to be true, and every attempt to deepen our knowledge of spiritual matters must carry with it a commitment to live out our newfound understandings. Jesus really said the same thing when He said, "If I had not come and spoken unto them, they had not had sin: but now they have no cloak [excuse] for their sin." (John 15:22) The point in both the readings and the Bible is the same: We are held accountable for what we know. Not that we must perfectly live everything we know to be right, but that we have a responsibility to do our best to behave in ways that are consistent with what we know to be right. If our behavior does not come close to our knowledge of right and wrong, the discrepancy is an extremely dangerous one for our spiritual health.

Symbolic interpretation, applied properly and allowed to unfold naturally from the literal story, serves only to enrich our understanding of the Bible's message for us. Approached arbitrarily or used as an exercise in spiritual-intellectual gymnastics, it is best left alone. This is why the third level of interpretation, that of practical application, is so very important.

The Level of Practical Application

On the level of practical application, the stories in the Bible not only give us symbolic insights concerning inner states of heart and mind, but they also give us concrete instruction on how to behave. In other words, the people in the Bible serve as examples for us. Now this is an area where the Bible will sometimes fall under fire. Skeptics will point to some of the terrible events that took place, particularly during Old Testament times, and question how such a record could be considered the word of God. Yet they sometimes overlook the fact that we can learn some of the best lessons from some of the worst examples. Take the story of Cain. From the story of the first murderer, we can learn a lesson that could transform this world.

What We Can Learn from the Story of Cain. As we read in the Book of Genesis, Cain murders his brother, Abel, out of jealousy. When God later questions Cain concerning his brother's whereabouts, he casually answers, "Am I my brother's keeper?" (Genesis 4:9) In the events that follow, it is made very clear that Cain was indeed his brother's keeper. Now if we were to take that principle, "I am my brother's keeper," and apply it—live it—in every human contact for just one day, it would probably transform our lives. If *all* of us could do it on the *same* day, it would transform this globe. So from a bad example, we can learn a very good lesson on the practical level.

What We Can Learn from the Story of David. King David of the Old Testament is a marvelous practical example for us to follow. The Bible tells us that David's heart was "perfect with the Lord his God . . . " (I Kings 15:3) That was easy enough for me to understand when I was very young and just learning about David in Sunday school. The story of the idealistic young shepherd anointed king of Israel and the account of how the young David conquered the giant Goliath with just his slingshot were consistent with the hero figure. But when I got a little older and read more deeply into David's life, I discovered—to my horror—that David committed at one time or another just about every sin imaginable.

I must admit that this created a bit of confusion for me. It did not seem fair that someone who did all of the things David did should go down in Bible history as such a sterling character. It seemed that much more was expected of me in the way of obedience to God's will, and I wasn't even a Bible hero! Then I came across an Edgar Cayce reading that made the point of David's example clear to me. It said that the important thing about David was not that he sinned, but that he repented. (5753-2) The reading stressed the true meaning of repentance—not just the shedding of crocodile tears and then going one's merry way, but a sincere commitment to "turn around," to not repeat the mistake.

In the light of this insight, David's life became for me a statement concerning God's unfailing mercy. In David's actions we see repeated reminders of the ever-present potential for renewal. David's many sins were not the important part of his story. The important part, the example for us to follow, is that David always picked up the pieces and tried again. The message for us is that no matter how badly we may go astray, no matter how we may depart from the spiritual path, our God is a merciful and forgiving God who will have us back if that is what we ask.

As the Edgar Cayce readings gently admonish, when we fall short of our ideals, the issue to focus on is not whether we stumble, but whether we try again. There was a woman who asked repeatedly in her reading why she was "failing" in various aspects of her life. The answer given was, "You have not failed *yet*. You only fail if you quit trying!" (3292-1) David is a wonderful example of one who never quit trying, and for that he went down in the biblical record as one whose heart was perfect before God.

The Bible's Practical Examples Run the Gamut from the First Murderer to the Perfect Son of God. Finally, on the practical level of Bible interpretation, we have the supreme example of Jesus. Certainly, the readings of Edgar Cayce deal with Jesus as far more than just an example. We have touched on the complexity of the Cayce readings concerning Jesus in both the section on Jesus and the section on reincarnation. But for our exploration of the practical level of Bible interpretation, let's focus on the practical value of Jesus' example. If we are to view the biblical accounts as examples for our instruction, then there is no example more important than that of Jesus. For in His perfection, He gave us a blueprint for living. It has been suggested that at any decisional point concerning conduct, we need only ask, "What would Jesus do?" in order to know what is right. In working with the practical level of Bible interpretation, that is exactly what we would do. If from Cain's bad example we can learn a lesson, how much more can we learn from heeding the example of the perfect Son of God?

A Summary of the Three Levels of Interpretation

We can see, then, how the three levels of Bible interpretation work together to present a whole and balanced approach to Scripture. Rooted in the literal, the Cayce approach is protected from the pitfalls that may come from an arbitrary and purely subjective interpretation of the Bible. The readings' emphasis on the literal and historical also serves to remind us that the Bible is the record of how God is active in history, interceding in the affairs of mankind. Exploring the Bible stories in the readings, we find the biblical accounts supported and the inspiration of those events brought home to us anew.

Then, moving to the symbolic level, we can use our understanding of what literally took place to suggest that passage's symbolic significance. It is on the symbolic level that we apply the message of Scripture to our own inner being and claim its story as our own. It is on the level of practical application that we take those symbolic insights and put them to work. For on the practical level we go on to manifest or live out the lessons of Scripture.

If this three-level approach to the Bible doesn't seem like anything particularly new or unusual, now that we have examined it step by step, that is because it isn't! In essence, every preacher uses the three steps when giving a Sunday morning sermon: First, a chosen passage of Scripture is read and explored. Various aspects of the literal story are explained. Then the congregation will be told of how this same story applies to them, as they sit there in the pews. Finally, the preacher will make behavioral admonitions based on the Bible passage at hand. This is exactly the essence of the Cayce readings' three-level approach to Bible interpretation.

No, Edgar Cayce did not seem to advocate an especially occult view of the Bible. What he did advocate, however, was daily reading of it and a commitment to live by its message. For countless people, this emphasis in the Cayce material has meant a return to their Bibles and the churches they had abandoned years before discovering Cayce. In case after case, the readings' suggestions for working with the Bible have returned people to the mainstream of Christianity. (See Appendix B.) How are Cayce's suggestions implemented? In the next chapter we will build on the theoretical framework of the three-level approach to develop a practical plan for working with the Bible on a daily basis.

16

A Plan for Working with the Bible

THE BIBLE IS a perennial bestseller. Yet so often, once the book has been purchased, it will lie on a shelf somewhere collecting dust. We can ask ourselves why this happens. Was the person who purchased the Bible insincere? That seems unlikely. The individual who deliberately sets out to obtain a Bible is obviously looking for something. Inspiration, an understanding of life, a sense of relatedness to God, a code for living—all of these are possible motivations behind that original acquisition of a Bible. Can we conclude, then, that some sincere seekers are disappointed in the Bible because it fails in some way to live up to its reputation? The vital role the Bible

FREE CATALOG OF BOOKS AND MEMBERSHIP ACTIVITIES

Fill-in and mail this postage-paid card today.

Please write clearly

Name: _____

Address: _____

City: _____

State/Province: _____

Postal/Zip Code: _____ Country: _____

458-5
7/99

Association for Research and Enlightenment, Inc.
215 67th Street
Virginia Beach, VA 23451-2061

For Faster Service call 1-800-723-1112
www.are-cayce.com

BUSINESS REPLY MAIL

FIRST CLASS   PERMIT NO. 2456   VIRGINIA BEACH, VA

POSTAGE WILL BE PAID BY ADDRESSEE

ASSOCIATION FOR RESEARCH
AND ENLIGHTENMENT INC
215 67TH STREET
VIRGINIA BEACH VA 23451-9819

plays in millions of lives is evidence enough that *this* is not true. To what, then, can we attribute the widespread tendency not to use the Bible on a regular basis?

Using a Theme for Understanding

One possibility is that there is often a gap between the life-changing potential of the Bible and the reader's tools for understanding it. Another way to express this would be to say that the Bible is as real and alive as the theme or understanding with which we read it. For example, the historian can read the Bible in the light of his or her specialized knowledge, and it will come alive as a history to be compared and contrasted with other histories. The reader of wide literary knowledge can explore the Bible as a piece of literature, seeing and appreciating aspects that would totally escape the reader without such a background. Likewise, the person with a particular set of beliefs will often find that the Bible comes alive only within the framework of those beliefs. It has been said that a person who knows only one language knows none. It is this same principle which suggests that it is helpful to have a framework in which to place our study of the Bible, for the framework becomes the other "language" that helps bring out the depth and meaning in the original.

The following framework is based on the three levels of interpretation discussed in the last chapter. It also draws on Edgar Cayce's many references to daily Bible study. It is offered not as the one, definitive approach to working with the Bible, but as one of many possible approaches. Because it seems to be the approach most consistent with the Cayce readings and because it has been so helpful to countless students of the Bible, I include it here as the last chapter of *Edgar Cayce and Christian Faith*. After all, for one whose Christian faith acknowledges the authority of Scripture, the Bible is a necessary part of life. And for anyone who chooses to work seriously with *all* of the Edgar Cayce readings, the admonition to use the Bible is rather difficult to ignore.

Choosing a Version to Study

For the biblically centered Christian, of course, faith in Jesus is the condition that unlocks the message of Scripture. It may seem presumptuous to suggest that there is anything other than the power of the Holy Spirit Himself that can make the Bible come alive. Yet it is the Bible itself that the Spirit often works through to lead people to faith in Christ. Some plan of study may, therefore, be important prior to faith. Even for the person of established Christian faith, it can be difficult at times to know where to begin studying the Bible and more difficult still to understand its words once the study is begun; hence, the great assortment of Bible translations and paraphrases, a condition that can be very confusing to the person wanting to study the "right" version of the Bible. Edgar Cayce was asked more than once to tell which version of the Bible was the accurate one. His responses are a bit eye-opening.

> For, much might be given respecting that *ye* have that *ye* call the Bible. This has passed through many hands. Many that would turn that which was written into the meanings that would suit their own purposes, as ye yourselves often do. But if ye will get the spirit of that written there ye may find it will lead thee to the gates of heaven . . . Read it to be wise. Study it to understand. *Live* it to know that the Christ walks through same with thee. 262-60

When, in another place, Edgar Cayce was asked,

"What present printed version of the Bible gives the nearest to the true meaning of both the New and Old Testaments?" he answered:

> The nearest true version for the entity is that ye apply of whatever version ye read, in your life. It isn't that ye learn from anyone. Ye only may have the direction. The learning, the teaching is within self. For where hath He promised to meet thee? Within the temple! Where is that temple? Within! Where is heaven or earth? Within! Meet thy Savior there . . .
>
> There have been many versions of that which was purposed to have been written, and has been changed from all of those versions—but remember that the whole gospel of Jesus Christ is: "Thou shalt love the Lord thy God with all thy mind, thy heart and thy body; and thy neighbor as thyself." Do this and thou shalt have eternal life. The rest of the book is trying to describe that. It is the same in any language . . . 2072-14

Finally, one asked whether the Lord's Prayer is correct as given in the Bible and "If not, would appreciate it as was given by the Master to the disciples," the response was:

> This may be given, but rather should the seeker use that which *is* given—as the Lord calls on all to do . . . For, there be many misinterpretations, poor translations, but to find fault with that thou hast and not use same is to make excuses that you haven't it as it was given. 281-20

These excerpts suggest that sometimes we use the uncertainty over Bible translations as an excuse not to work with the Bible at all. Always practical in their approach, the readings counter such excuses with the reminder that it's best to just choose one version and then work with it. To begin with, it makes sense to choose a version with language you can understand. If the archaic language of the King James or one of the other older versions is an obstacle to your reading comprehension, then by all means choose a modern translation. If, on the other hand, you find beauty in the language of the King James that has evocative power for you, then work with that version. Remember that all Bible translations have been taken from manuscripts that are not "original" in themselves, but represent the best records we have of the originals. The important thing is to find a translation of the Bible that you are comfortable with and start working with it.

But where to begin working with it, once you've chosen your version of the Bible? The well-meaning seeker who allows his or her Bible to collect dust may well have once started Genesis 1:1 with the best of intentions; but somewhere around the middle of II Chronicles he or she bogged down and never resumed reading. How do we keep from becoming lost—or worse yet, bored—with some of the more confusing or repetitious portions of the Bible?

One antidote to this problem is to begin the study of Scripture with certain key passages, rather than attempt to read from cover to cover. Then later, as familiarity with Bible reading grows, go back and try the sequential, chronological approach. For those looking for a place to begin reading the Bible, there are some excellent suggestions in the Cayce readings.

Bible Passages Most Often Recommended in the Readings

Edgar Cayce recommended Bible reading for all sorts

of people. He recommended the Bible for people who were in inner turmoil. He recommended it for people who had physical problems and wanted to get well. He recommended it for business people. In all of these suggestions, we find three portions of Scripture recommended over and over again as the place to begin reading the Bible:

John 14-17. In these chapters of John's Gospel, we find the last words Jesus spoke to His disciples before His arrest and subsequent crucifixion. The readings advise us to read them, not just as the words spoken to the eleven who remained with Jesus in the Upper Room, but as words spoken directly to each one of us today. The promises, the reassurances, the spiritual admonitions expressed in those four chapters may be taken as Jesus' message to us personally.

Deuteronomy 30. This passage, perhaps less well known than the New Testament passage from John, is nonetheless a beautiful and extremely significant portion of Scripture. For in this chapter, we read the key issue facing humanity in the earth: "See, I have set before thee this day life and good, and death and evil . . . " (Deuteronomy 30:15) Free will. Our capacity, our *responsibility* to make choices is the thread running throughout our experience as spiritual beings living in a material world. Deuteronomy 30:15 serves to remind us of the choice that is before us every day.

This excerpt from Deuteronomy also carries the promise that God will not forsake Israel: "If any of thine be driven out unto the outmost parts of heaven, from thence will the Lord thy God gather thee, and from thence will he fetch thee . . . " (verse 4) Adding the symbolic understanding that Israel represents the seeker after truth (as discussed in chapter 15), we can accept this reassurance as our own—so long as we, too, are seekers after truth. This biblical chapter seems to be of key importance, then, because it reminds us of both our responsibility and God's care for us.

Exodus 20. It should not be too surprising that the third passage the Cayce readings most often recommended for study is the portion of Exodus that gives us the Ten Commandments. For the concept that there is a lawfulness to life and God's expectations of us is a familiar theme in all of the Cayce material. We considered this in some detail in chapters 12 and 14, first as we developed a definition of reincarnation and then again later as we traced the development of law and grace through the Bible. Given the Cayce readings' emphasis on application, living what we believe, it is no wonder that the readings pointed people to the Ten Commandments as an encapsulated code for living.

Taken as a unit, these three often-recommended Bible passages comprise almost a miniversion of the Bible's message for the human soul: God has provided a standard or spiritual code for living that is conducive to growth and spiritual health. (Exodus 20) Yet it is we who must choose life or death, good or evil. (Deuteronomy 30) Still, the reminder is there that it is not for us to travel our spiritual path alone, for in the words of Jesus we have not only the assurance of the Father's abiding love for us, but also Jesus' own saving power for the human soul. (John 14-17) It's easy to see, then, why these three passages are a good place to begin working with the Bible.

There are other portions of Scripture frequently mentioned and recommended in the Cayce readings as well. Among them are the 23rd Psalm, the fifth chapter of Matthew, and the twelfth chapter of Romans. These were just mentioned as recommendations, of course, for the important advice given repeatedly was to read, study, and live the Scripture.

Obviously, there is no lack of material to work with in studying the Bible. Even if one were to concentrate solely on the readings-recommended passages just listed, there would be food for a lifetime of study. But still, once one has selected a passage from the Bible—either by choice or at random—the task, then, of understanding that passage is not always easy. Here is where the three levels of interpretation come in.

Using the Three Levels of Interpretation

In the last chapter we looked at how the literal, symbolic, and practical levels of interpretation can work together. Let's now take the theoretical framework a step further to derive a step-by-step blueprint for Bible study. For those readers who wish to follow an actual Bible passage through these steps, I have selected Acts, chapter 10, as an example for us to consider. As part of each step, we will see how the instructions given may be applied to that passage.

Step One: Work with a Literal Understanding of the Passage. The first, and most important, step in working with a Bible passage is to be sure you understand what is happening in the story or account before you. If you are reading a Bible story that has a plot and characters, try to summarize the story in a few simple sentences. Ask yourself, "If I had to tell this story to another person, how would I tell it?" Try to become as clear as possible about the literal events in the story. If the passage you are studying does not involve a true plot (for example, it may be an Old Testament prophecy, one of Jesus' sermons, or one of the epistles), then focus on what is being literally stated, who is saying it, and to whom it is being said.

Example:

Acts 10 is the story of Cornelius, Roman centurion and the first Gentile on record to embrace Christianity. As the passage begins, we are told that Cornelius, a godly man, had a vision in which he was instructed to send for Simon Peter who was then in Joppa. He immediately called two of his servants and one of his soldiers and sent them to Joppa in search of Peter.

Peter, meanwhile, also had a vision while he was praying on the rooftop of the home where he was staying. In Peter's vision, a sheet is lowered from the sky, bearing all kinds of animals that under Jewish law are considered unclean. A voice nonetheless tells him to kill and eat from among these animals. When he protests, saying that he has never eaten anything that is common or unclean, the Lord responds by saying, "What God hath cleansed, that call not thou common." (verse 15) The vision was repeated three times before the sheet was drawn back up and, as Peter remained on the rooftop contemplating it, the spirit told him of the three men who were coming for him and advised him to accompany them.

Peter does go with Cornelius's messengers and, when he arrives at Cornelius's home in Caesarea, he finds that the Gentile has gathered a group of friends and relatives. Cornelius attempts to worship Peter, but Peter protests, saying that he is merely a man. He goes on to speak of his vision as his reason for violating the Jewish law that would prevent him from entering a Gentile's home, and asks Cornelius why he sent for him. Cornelius then tells Peter of his vision.

Peter realizes that God shows no partiality (verse 34) and immediately preaches the message of Christ. The Holy Spirit is poured out on all who hear the sermon, Jew and Gentile alike. The Gentiles are then baptized in the name of Jesus Christ.

Readers who are experienced in working with dreams will notice a marked similarity to many dream interpretation approaches. The importance of becoming thoroughly familiar with the literal before going on to other levels of understanding cannot be overstated, for it is in the literal that the basic message is comprehended. That basic message later serves as an anchor that will keep symbolic interpretations rooted and related to the original account, be it a dream or a Bible passage. Further, the literal level is usually so rich with information and insights in its own right that we cheat ourselves by passing over it too quickly to get on to other levels of interpretation.

An added dimension to the literal level may also be drawn from the Edgar Cayce readings in those instances where the readings report on a Bible story or the character in it. Cornelius is one character who did happen to appear in the life readings, as it turns out. In 1939, a fifty-seven-year-old man came to Edgar Cayce for a life reading. A prior life as none other than Cornelius, the Roman centurion, is listed for this man. I include excerpts of that reading here for the insights it offers on the literal level:

> One [incarnation], as we find—it stands out beyond the others; not merely because of its historical value in the experiences of man, but because of the changes and the activities wrought by the entity's taking such a stand in the face of oppositions that might have been a part of the experience. 1848-1

Here we're told that this experience as Cornelius was important not only because of the historical changes it made (presumably in the course of Christianity), but also because of the changes brought about in Cornelius's

own life and soul when he was willing to face the oppo-
sitions that might have come to a Roman official em-
bracing Christianity.

And it would be well were the entity to have the
history of that sojourn in its fullest extent—as
Cornelius, the first of the Roman officials to take an
open stand with the followers of the Nazarene.

The man who came to Edgar Cayce is advised to become as familiar as possible with the life as Cornelius,
apparently as a way to greater personal insight.

There the entity, through the associations with
those who had come in personal contact with the
man of Galilee, began his seeking—through prayer—
to know what was man's relationship to his Maker.
Then there was the receiving of the vision as the
warning that he, Cornelius, was to send for one that
would acquaint him with those truths which had
been proclaimed by that representative of the heavenly kingdom.
And those activities of the entity in accepting, in
experiencing the outpouring and the call through
the activity of the spirit of truth, made for that great
change which came in the governing of that land;
and the modifying of the authority of those who
were put in power through the activities of the au-
thorities in Rome; making it possible, with those of
its fellows, that there would come the great opportunities for man in every walk of life to become acquainted with those truths that are a part of man's
heritage through the promises of the Creative
Forces in man's experience.

This portion of the reading suggests that in accepting

and experiencing the outpouring of the Spirit, Cornelius became an influence that spread through the Roman political structure. We are reminded of the reference in Acts to Cornelius's gathering his friends and relatives to await Peter. It is not hard to imagine such a man being a major influence in the political structure of which he was a part. Cornelius and his "fellows" were then responsible for leading countless others to the awareness of what this reading calls "man's heritage through the promises" of God.

> Thus in the present may the entity, as one in authority, one in power, make for those activities in which there will be in the hearts of men and women *everywhere* the realization of the greater necessity, the greater need, the greater opportunity of the peoples becoming aware more and more of their need to turn again to those tenets, those truths; not because they are of that nature that would make men meek or lonely, but making them *strong* and meek *in* their *strength!* For *in* such comes the power and the ability of the entity from those experiences to not only lead and direct men of many a position or status, but to be a voice heard among the nations of the earth. 1848-1

The final paragraph of this excerpt suggests that the soul entity who was Cornelius has carried over into his twentieth-century life the authority and the power that make him a good ambassador for the truth Peter spoke in his sermon at Caesarea. Further, he is told that because of his status and his power, he is in a position to demonstrate that those truths do not foster weakness, but strength. We might speculate that Mr. 1848 was a businessman or politician who faced the challenge of incorporating spiritual principles into his professional life.

As in the other examples in which Edgar Cayce commented on events mentioned in the Bible, we find implicit acceptance of the story as reported in Scripture and further insights that are based on a knowledge of the biblical account. This approach is at the heart of literal interpretation, and it provides a good foundation for symbolic interpretation as well.

Step Two: Develop a Plausible Symbolic Interpretation. At this step, many people feel confounded. But usually this is because they believe that symbols are hidden and must somehow be "figured out." If, on the other hand, we let the literal story suggest the symbology, the task is a relatively easy one. Remember that, when trying to understand a Bible passage symbolically, we are looking for inner traits that a particular character and his or her story may suggest to us. In any given story, there may be several characters who hold symbolic messages for us, and so it is usually best to take these one at a time, trying to isolate the main character to work with first. The following points are good ones to consider when determining which states of consciousness a given character might represent:

- List the main characteristics you notice about this particular Bible character.
- What external factors (such as other people and circumstances) came to bear on this character's experience as reported in this Bible passage?
- Considering the plot in the literal story, try to pick out the choices that faced this character. What possible outcomes might have resulted from each choice? What did the character in fact decide and what were the consequences of that decision?
- What aspects of human consciousness do this character's choices and characteristics suggest?

• Now see if you can suggest a symbolic interpretation of this Bible passage.

Example:

While both Cornelius and Peter play key roles in this story, let's consider Cornelius the main character and answer the questions above with respect to him:

• *We are told that Cornelius was devout. We can also see that he was obedient and unafraid when it came to heeding God. We also know that he was generous, for he "gave much alms to the people . . . " (verse 2) He was willing to act on faith, too, for he gathered a group to hear Peter even before Peter's arrival.*

• *Peter, the apostle of the Lord, is probably the strongest external factor that came to bear on Cornelius. Peter's coming and subsequent preaching and baptizing were all factors that interacted with Cornelius. Even Cornelius's original vision may in one sense be seen as an external factor that came to bear on him.*

• *Several choices faced Cornelius. Even before this story begins, Cornelius had made certain choices concerning the kind of life he would live. It is clear that he was a man of strong moral and spiritual character. Once he had the vision, Cornelius had the choice to heed it or not. Had he not sent for Peter, the course of the spread of Christianity might have been different. He had the choice to act quickly or to delay. Had he delayed, Peter's own location and experience might not have dovetailed so perfectly with Cornelius's. So Cornelius also had the choice to pursue his vision timidly and quietly or to gather his friends and relatives to hear Peter's message. The descent of the Holy Spirit might not have been so overpoweringly convincing had there not been a large group there that day.*

• *In short, we might say that Cornelius represented*

the human consciousness that is first open to guidance from God and then ready to act on that guidance, despite the odds and despite our customs and institutions. He is unafraid to stand up for his beliefs.

• *To interpret this story symbolically, we would probably want also to consider Peter in the light of the points above, for this experience in learning that what God had cleansed should not be called unclean is one of the main points of the story. We might briefly say that Peter symbolized the consciousness that was grounded in the accepted and lawful, yet was open to fresh guidance from God. This trait enabled him to catch a larger vision and recognize that Christianity was not just a sect of Judaism, but open to all of mankind.*

The symbology of this story might suggest, then, that if we are first obedient to what we know of God's will and honestly seek His further leading, He will guide us in ways that go beyond our expectations or our vision of the possible.

Step Three: Look for Ways to Apply Your Symbolic Understanding. Remembering that we are responsible to live what we know, it is important to take any study of the Bible to the level of practical application. The goal at this level is to find specific ways that the passage's message can be lived in your own life. A good way to begin this process is to use the symbolic interpretation to come up with the "moral of the story." From the time we were children, we have heard tales that end with "And the moral of the story is . . . "; and most times the moral is fairly clear with just a minimum of consideration. Once having worked through the literal and symbolic levels of a Bible story, the moral is usually quite discernible there as well.

For example, we could say that the moral of the story of

Cornelius is, "First practice what you know to be in accordance with God's will. Then continue to seek guidance from Him in life's concerns. Be open to God's leading and do not reject the form His leading takes just because it is not what you might have anticipated."

The last, and most crucial, step is for each individual to find personal applications of that moral. These applications should be concrete and based on current conditions in life, rather than vague and general statements. To the extent that we emerge from our Bible study with sweeping principles, we will be less likely to put them into practice. If, however, we take time to see how these principles can be applied in the day-by-day challenges of life, we are far more likely to live them out.

To apply the moral of the Cornelius story, for example, one person might decide to recommit to a regular period of prayer and meditation. Another might decide to consider a new idea prayerfully rather than reject it out-of-hand. Still someone else might learn from Cornelius's example to not be afraid to give voice to his or her beliefs.

Regardless of the personal application chosen, most Bible students will find that these three steps—or any approach that leads to making the Bible a part of daily living—will be well worth the time spent on them.

A Challenge to Experiment

Finally, in encouraging people to work with the Bible, Edgar Cayce suggested that we " . . . read a portion of scripture—not haphazardly but regularly as a routine, daily, and there will come those unfoldments in the daily experience." (3328-1) As they did so often, the readings were once again encouraging the "try it and see" attitude, even an experimental approach. Never did the readings present information to be accepted wholesale, just because Edgar Cayce said it. The suggestion, instead, was to experiment with the information, to try it and see if it improved any aspect of life, to see if it rang true against the standards of one's beliefs and ideals.

It was in this spirit of adventure and experiment that the readings encouraged us to read a portion of Scripture every day and watch for the "unfoldments" in our daily lives. They didn't say what those "unfoldments" would be. They merely challenged us to try it and see what happens. What have we got to lose?

Appendix A

Edgar Cayce Readings on Jesus the Christ

... HE IS THE rock of salvation ...

... "Though ye wander far afield, though ye become beset by the doubts and the fears, though ye even turn thy back upon *me,* if ye will remember the promises and *turn,* I *will hear—speedily—*and will forgive thy trespasses, even as *you* forgive those that trespass against you."

Let love be without dissimulation. Look not upon that which may bring only joy to thee, yet even peace to thee; for He is thy light and thy guide. Put rather thy life, thy *experiences,* thy associations, even thine own self, into His keeping; knowing He

is able to keep that thou has committed unto Him—
and may save thee, for He alone hath the words of
life. And no matter what ye make or mark, or mar,
He is *still* with thee, ready to harken when ye call.

Let thine heart be raised, then, in praise that thou
hast *named* the Name above every other name; for
He alone can save—and He alone can *forgive*—He
alone can answer prayer; to the same measure that
thou, in thine own experience, *answereth* the prayer
of thy fellow man. 262-75

. . . ye are secure and safe in the promises of
Him—who *is* the Prince of Peace—not of the world
as the world knows the world, but He that *overcame*
the world! And so may ye overcome the world—in
His promises. 1971-1

For, as given, the greatest service to God is service to his creatures; for, as shown in the Holy One,
without spot or blemish, yet gave Himself that others through Him might have the advocate to the
approach to the Father without fear; in that He had
passed through the flesh and the rules of the
earthly, fleshly existence, taking on all the weaknesses of the flesh, yet never abusing, never misus-
ing, never misconstruing, never giving to others a
wrong impression of the knowledge of the universe;
never giving any save loving brotherhood . . .
254-17

For ye know, ye understand—all stand as one before Him. There are no ones above another; only
those that do His will. What is His will? "Thou shalt
love the Lord with all thy heart, thy mind, thy
body—and thy neighbor as thyself." This is the
whole law—the spiritual law, the mental law, the

material law. And as ye apply same, thus ye become the *law!* For as He, thy Master, thy Lord, thy Christ fulfilled the law by compliance with same, He became the law and thus thy Savior, thy Brother, thy Christ! 1662-1

Then indeed may there be a glimpse of the love the Father hath shown to the children of men, through the very gift of Him, thy Brother, the Christ; that we may walk circumspectly one with another; and thus give, show forth, *His* activity in the earth till we be made as one with Him, in the glories that were His and that are as He has given for us. For we be joint heirs, as one with Him; not strangers, not aliens but joint heirs with the Christ to the kingdom of the Father—that is, that was, that ever shall be—even before the foundations of the earth were laid . . .

For His heart ached, yea His body was sore and weary; yea His body bled not only from the nail prints in His hands and feet but from the spear thrust into the heart of hearts! For the blood as of the perfect man was shed, not by reason of Himself but that there might be made an offering once for all; that then *ye* may know, ye in thine own self are not a burden to any.

For with thy mind, thy heart, ye may give much, much the more to those about thee in their ministry to thy physical weaknesses; that the very glory of Him may be manifested in their lives.

For if we do good only to those that would do good to us, what praise, what profit is there in same? For it was the unjustness of His trial, the persecutions of His body, that made the way for mankind, ye His brethren, ye thy own self, to *have* and know the way that leads to "That peace I leave with thee;

not as the world knoweth peace, but my peace I give," in that:

Though ye be hindered, though ye be misunderstood, yea though ye be persecuted for those things that are not even thine *own* faults—how much greater is the manifestation of His glory for that which was a shortcoming in thee to be made right in ministering good unto others through the love He hath shown to thee? 1504-1

As given, without the shedding of blood there was no remission of sin. As given in the beginning of man's concept of making atonement for the wrongs done self in relationship to the Creative Forces.

For, the error that man makes is the more oft against himself than making for the breaking of law as related to divine influence in the experience. For, love is law—law is love, in its essence. And with the breaking of the law is the making of the necessity for atonement and forgiveness, in that which may take away error to or what has been brought in the experience of the individual.

Hence the shedding of blood in the *man* Jesus made for the atoning for *all* men, through making Himself in at-onement with the law and with love. For, through *love* was brought the desire to make self and His brother in at-onement. Hence in the atoning or shedding of the blood comes the redemption to man, through that which may make for *his*—man's—at-onement—with Him. 262-45

Then, as we have indicated again and again— that which has been found good in the experience of many should be presented; in a way as to give the opportunities for others, too, to know that they are children of the Most High God, and that there *is* an access to Him—through the simple, unostentatious life as was manifested in His Son, Jesus, the Christ . . .

Not a new doctrine—not even a new thought; but rather showing that there *is* something that each individual can do *about* the fact that Jesus the Christ is the way! Wherever the individual is, or no matter in what position in life he may be. 254-108

Appendix B

Edgar Cayce Readings on the Church

(Q) WHAT IS the Holy Church?

(A) That which makes for the awareness in the heart of the individual. It is as He that was set as the head of the Church is the church. The Church is never a body, never an assembly. An *individual* soul becomes aware that it has taken that Head, that Son, that Man even, to be the intermediator. *That* is the Church; that is what is spoken of as the Holy Church.

What readest thou? "Upon this I will build my church."

What church? The Holy Church? Who is the head?

That One upon whom the conditions had been set by that question asked. For here ye may find the answer again to many of those questions sought concerning the Spirit, the Church, the Holy Force that manifests by the attuning of the individual; though it may be for a moment. He asked, "Whom say men that I am?" Then Peter answered, "Thou art the Christ, the son of the living God!" Then, "Upon this I will build my church, and the gates of hell shall not prevail against it." He said to Peter, "Flesh and blood—*flesh* and blood—hath not revealed this unto thee, but my Father which is in heaven." Heaven? Where? Within the hearts, the minds; the place where Truth is made manifest! Wherever Truth is made manifest it gives place to that which is heaven *for those that seek* and love truth! but a mighty hell for those that seek gratification of their own selves! And these are those things which become stumblingblocks to many an individual that becomes more and more material-minded. For there must be seen; yet they heed not what *has* been seen and heard and given of old. Who communicated, ye want to know, to Peter when he gave this confession? Whom did He say is thy father, thy mother, thy sister, thy brother? He that doeth the will of the Father in heaven, the same is thy *earthly* father, thy *earthly* mother, thy earthly brother and thy sister. They that love *truth* rather than the satisfying, the gratifying of *fleshly* desires. This does not indicate that no beauty, no joy, no happiness is to be in the experience of those who claim to seek to be the channel of blessings, or the source of inspiration to others! Who is the father of Joy? Who is the father of Happiness? Who is the father of Peace? The same that thou would serve in showing forth the Lord's death till He come again. For he that is long-faced, he that is sorry for the world is sorry most for himself; and of such has He said, "Though in my name ye cast out demons, though ye heal the sick, I will say Depart from me, I never knew you." Why? For ye have your own glory when such is done that it may be seen and known and heard among men alone.

But love thy neighbor. Love thine enemy. Love those that despitefully use you. For what profit hath thou if ye love only those that love you? 262-87

(Q) With what church would it be well for me to seek affiliation at this time?
(A) The better is the church within self, not by name or place. For the church is the living Christ. Make association first with that, and whether it is in this, that or the other name, Christ ye serve and not a church! 2823-3

(Q) Am I the chosen channel for the enlargement of Methodism in more vital, Christian relationships, as given through the call of the W.E.C.?
(A) A channel. Few would choose to be *the* channel. For, *the* channel must be *Him*. But as a representative of Him in such a service, *well* chosen. Well to magnify, not any cult or denomination—for Christ is Lord of all. Through that organization, well—but magnify the Christ, *not* the method. 2574-1

(Q) Should I affiliate with any particular church organization?
(A) A particular church organization is well. For it centers the mind. But don't get the idea that you have the whole cheese. 3350-1

(Q) How can this group best meet the conditions that have arisen in relation to the Church?

(A) Do the lessons not make the individuals that are members of individual churches *better* Christians, better or nearer Christ-like; thus filling their lives with such love that dogmatic principles (as in some churches) must be taboo? But present them to those that are weak, *living* them before those that *stumble*—but do not cram them down anyone's throat! Neither argue with them! Did thy Master ever argue, even when there were the greater railings or abuses? He presented that which each *has* found, did find, convicted them. What said He respecting that? "I do not condemn thee, for thou art condemned already in thine own self." So, in the approach to those influences, the truths and lessons as presented—and *lived* by individuals—should fill the needs, even in the greater or higher places in any individual organization; and may fill some with awe—and they may speak evil. So did the High Priest condemn thine Lord! So did those of the Sanhedrin wreak their own purposes upon Him. Yea, art thou willing to live that which has proved and does prove in thine experience that which makes thee closer with thy God? If these lessons are not founded in such, have nothing to do with them. 262-61

Appendix C

Why Read the Bible?

... READ A PORTION of scripture—not haphazardly but regularly as a routine, daily, and there will come those unfoldments in the daily experience. 3328-1

In the physical forces to assist the body in gaining this, more time must be given to the study of the Holy Word, and more expression of self must be spent in manifesting those truths before men. 3981-1

But study to know thy relationship to thy Creator.

No better handbook may be used than the Scripture itself. 1966-1

. . . that what . . . trouble there may arise in the life of the entity, in social, marital, home, business, or what not, that the dependence of the Book, the lessons, the truths, the exposition of the manifestation of the Holy Spirit in the earth's forces, is ever the Guide to everyone. 900-232

Read the Book, if you would get educated. If you would be refined, live it! If you would be beautiful, practice it in thy daily life! 3647-1

In the mental attitudes we would hold to those that have been indicated for constructive influences. And if this is done in a prayerful, meditative manner, following the suggestions that have been indicated as portions of the Holy Writ as should be not just memorized but realized as a living experience in the application of self in relationships to its home, to its friends, to its neighbors, to even its passing acquaintances—we will find it will not only aid materially . . . but will make the whole outlook upon life and its activities much more, not tolerable but much more worth while! 1773-3

Live and keep normal activities. Begin with the study of self—not anatomically but spiritually. And the greater spiritual lesson you may gain is in the 5th chapter of Matthew. Learn this by heart, then read the 14th chapter of John and the 12th chapter of Romans. Then live them! Live them in thy daily relationships to others. Know that these words are spoken to thee. Apply these with thy application of the mechanical and material things for the body. 3364-1

Notes

Chapter Two

1. I do not feel I can make passing reference to this practice of opening the Bible at random for guidance without adding some commentary concerning it. This was a practice that I had more or less happened upon on my own, though I later learned that others have used it and that there is some disagreement among Christians as to the appropriateness of this approach. Some believe that if we sincerely pray for guidance and then open the Bible at random, prepared to take whatever advice we find there, God will speak to us in this way. I certainly believed this at the time I used this method and have no doubt that the example given above, as well as some others that will come later, are genuine cases of answered prayer. In each instance, there was a rather uncanny matching of scriptural passage with the question on my mind at the time.

However, other Christians disparage this practice, calling it "Bible roulette." In my own life, I have stopped using this method of obtaining guidance, as I found that a reliance on it can retard growth in other methods of obtaining inner guidance. For me, it eventually threatened to lure me into a kind of lazy passivity in which I expected answers to come without my taking the trouble to cultivate an ear for the "still, small voice" within. As a result, the practice of obtaining guidance from a random reading of the Bible stopped working for me.

DISCOVER HOW THE EDGAR CAYCE MATERIAL CAN HELP YOU!

The Association for Research and Enlightenment, Inc. (A.R.E.®), was founded in 1931 by Edgar Cayce. Its international headquarters are in Virginia Beach, Virginia, where thousands of visitors come year-round. Many more are helped and inspired by A.R.E.'s local activities in their own hometowns or by contact via mail (and now the Internet!) with A.R.E. headquarters.

People from all walks of life, all around the world, have discovered meaningful and life-transforming insights in the A.R.E. programs and materials, which focus on such areas as holistic health, dreams, family life, finding your best vocation, reincarnation, ESP, meditation, personal spirituality, and soul growth, in small-group settings. Call us today on our toll-free number

1-800-333-4499

or

Explore our electronic visitor's center on the
INTERNET: **http://www.are-cayce.com**

We'll be happy to tell you more about how the work of the A.R.E. can help you!

A.R.E.
215 67th Street
Virginia Beach, VA 23451-2061